A Practical Guide for Key Stage 4

edited by
John Foster and Gordon Dennis

Stanley Thornes (Publishers) Ltd

Text © John Foster and Gordon Dennis 1997

Artwork by Richard Barton

Original line illustrations © Stanley Thornes (Publishers) Ltd 1997

The right of Gordon Dennis and John Foster to be identified as authors of this work has been asserted by them in accordance with the Copyright, Designs and Patents Act 1988.

All rights reserved. No part of this publication may be reproduced or transmitted in any form or by any means, electronic or mechanical, including photocopy, recording or any information storage and retrieval system, without permission in writing from the publisher or under licence from the Copyright Licensing Agency Limited. Further details of such licences (for reprographic reproduction) may be obtained from the Copyright Licensing Agency Limited, of 90 Tottenham Court Road, London W1P 9HE.

First published in 1997 by:
Stanley Thornes (Publishers) Ltd
Ellenborough House
Wellington Street
CHELTENHAM GL50 1YW
England

97 98 99 00 01 / 10 9 8 7 6 5 4 3 2 1

A catalogue record for this book is available from the British Library.

ISBN 0–7487–2982–8

Acknowledgements

The author and publishers would like to thank the following for permission to reproduce copyright material.

Paul Berry, Literary Executor for the Estate of the author for Vera Brittain, 'The Lament of the Demobilized' from *Poems of the War and After*, Gollancz, 1934 and *Verses of a VAD*, Imperial War Museum, 1995; Carcanet Press Ltd for Hugh MacDiarmid, 'Another Epitaph on Army of Mercenaries' from *Collected Poems*, Macmillan 1962; Macmillan Publishers Ltd for Thomas Hardy 'Drummer Hodge' from *The Collected Poems of Thomas Hardy*, Papermac 1976; and with Mrs Gibson for Wilfred Gibson, 'Ambulance Train' from *Collected Poems (1905–1925)*, 1926; Oxford University Press for Robert Bridges, 1936; George Sassoon for 'Suicide in the Trenches' and 'Reconciliation' from *Collected Poems of Siegfried Sassoon (1908–1956)*, Faber 1961; The Society of Authors on behalf of the Estate of A E Housman for A E Housman, 'On Wenlock Edge' and 'Epitaph on an Army of Mercenaries' from *The Collected Poems of A E Housman*, Jonathan Cape 1960; A P Watt Ltd on behalf of Michael Yeats for W B Yeates, 'The Wild Swans at Coole' and 'An Irishman Foresees his Death' from *The Collected Poems of W B Yeats*, Macmillan 1952.

Page 170: FIT83192 P.125–19503. pt 39 The Sick Rose: plate 39 from *Songs of Innocence and of Experience* (Copy AA) c.1815–26 (etching, ink and w/c) by William Blake (1757–1827). Fitzwilliam Museum, University of Cambridge/Bridgeman Art Library, London.

Every effort has been made to trace all the copyright holders; but if any have been inadvertently overlooked, the author and publishers will be pleased to amend further printings.

Typeset by Tech-Set, Gateshead, Tyne & Wear
Printed and bound in Great Britain at Scotprint Ltd, Musselburgh, Scotland

Contents

Time and Place

Reflections

Introduction

Thornes Classic Poetry: A Practical Guide for Key Stage 4 provides a course which is suitable for students aged 14 to 16 preparing for their GCSE or Standard Grade examinations. The term 'classic poetry' is taken to mean not only poems by pre-twentieth-century poets, but also poems written in the first two decades of the twentieth century which have stood the test of time and which, therefore, appear on the lists of prescribed authors. A key feature of the course is the inclusion of a substantial number of poems by women poets. Thus, the selection meets both the requirements of the National Curriculum and of the GCSE English and English Literature syllabuses.

The poems are presented in five sections, focusing on themes that are often highlighted because of their appropriateness to Key Stage 4. The thematic approach also offers opportunities for students to compare and contrast the way in which the themes are treated in different poems. The five sections are: Relationships, Conflict, People, Time and Place, and Reflections. The poems in each section are arranged according to subject-matter and style, rather than chronologically. However, for those teachers who wish to present the poems in an order which shows the historical development of English poetry, there is an index at the back of the book which lists the poets chronologically.

Each poem is introduced in a similar way with background notes providing information about the poet and about the poem. The aim of these notes is, first, to introduce the poet by giving brief interesting biographical details about their life and, second, to present any essential information about the historical and cultural context in which the poem was written. In a number of cases such notes provide an insight into the circumstances which prompted the writing of the poem, but it is important to stress to the students that the poem need not be interpreted historically and that a modern response and interpretation is perfectly valid. The purpose of these background notes is both to provide support that will assist a student's first reading of the poem and, where appropriate, to draw attention to particular features of the poem's structure and style. Further support is given in the notes after each poem, which gloss unfamiliar words and references.

Each poem is followed by suggestions for activities designed to encourage a personal response and to foster an understanding not only of the poem's contents, but also of its structure and the techniques used by the poet to achieve particular effects. Each activities section begins with a discussion and notemaking activity involving close textual study. Each student should be encouraged to take notes during the initial discussion and to amend the notes during any follow-up group or whole class discussion. The notes can then be referred to when tackling any of the writing suggestions, developing a piece of coursework or revising for the examination. Advice for students on how to take notes is given on page 5.

The initial activity is followed by suggestions for speaking and listening and/or writing. The speaking and listening activities range from preparing a reading of the poem to 'hotseating' and role plays. Advice for students on how to prepare a reading of a poem is given on pages 5–6. Some of the writing suggestions involve imaginative responses, such as diary and letter-writing, designed to help the students to fix in their minds the ideas presented in the poem. Other writing activities involve more formal essay-style answers that can be set for coursework or as practice for the examination.

At the end of each section there is a section overview containing examination-style questions which ask the students to explore how the language, structure and forms of different poems contribute to their meanings, to comment on the similarities and differences between poems written by the same poet, and to compare and contrast the style and structure of different poems on the same theme.

The book is designed to assist students to understand and respond to the poems. Throughout, both in the introductory notes to each poem and in the follow-up activities, attention is drawn to the form and structure of each poem and to any particular language features that occur in it. Students are introduced to poetic forms such as couplets, sonnets and blank verse, and to rhythm, metre and the effects achieved by poetic devices such as simile, metaphor, alliteration and personification. To help students, all technical terms appear in bold at their first mention and are explained in the glossary at the end of the book. In addition, some of these terms are also defined within the text itself in the context of a particular poem, with cross references where appropriate to enable students to locate them without difficulty.

To the Student

As you study the poems in this book, you will often be expected to make notes. You may also be asked to perform a poem by reading it aloud. Here are some guidelines to help you with these activities.

Notemaking

The notes you are asked to make fall into two main types – your first responses, and your second thoughts.

Your first responses should consist of jottings noting down any key words and phrases that strike you immediately after your first reading of the poem, your initial ideas of what the poem is about, anything that strikes you about its form or its language, and anything that puzzles you. The aim of these notes is to identify points in the poem that you will want to discuss or find out. Some people find that the easiest way to note their initial responses is to make a copy of the poem and to make notes around the poem, for example, by underlining key words and phrases, jotting down the associations that particular words suggest and putting question marks alongside lines that they do not understand. Other people prefer to write the title of the poem in the centre of a page and to draw a spidergram of their ideas, or simply to make a numbered list of points on a sheet of file paper. Whatever method you use, making these jottings will help you to begin to think about the poem and to work out its meaning.

The other type of notes you will be asked to make need to be more detailed and more organised, since these are the notes that you will want to use when writing coursework essays or for revision. Often you will be asked to make these notes during a pair or group discussion. The structure of the notes will frequently be dictated by the questions that you are asked. The questions may be organised so that you study the poem line by line or stanza by stanza. In such cases you can organise your notes on the poem using the sections of the poem as headings. As you are making these notes, while you are still engaged in the process of discussing the poem and working out its meaning, be prepared to add to them or to alter them when you share your ideas with other pairs or groups.

Sometimes, the notes that you make during your discussions will be sufficiently detailed for you to feel confident that you have included all the key points about the poem and that you will be able to revise from them without reorganising them. At other times, however, you will need to re-work them before filing them into your folder. A useful way of re-working your notes is to organise your ideas using the following headings: form, language, imagery and symbols, tone, theme.

Reading poetry aloud

When you are preparing to present either a reading or a performance of a poem, you must first study the poem in order to understand its meaning and the pattern its words make, line by line or stanza by stanza. You then have to decide what impression you want your reading to convey, and to consider how to present your interpretation to an audience. You will have to answer the following questions:

- How many speakers do you need? If there is more than one speaker, how are you going to divide the lines between the speakers?
- If there are changes in the mood of the poem, how are you going to show them? What should be the pace of the reading, and what should be its tone?

- Where should you pause during your reading? Where should there be short pauses and where should there be long pauses?
- Which words and phrases should you stress? At which point(s) in your reading should you either raise or lower the pitch of your voice (intonation)?

To help them to rehearse and perfect a reading of a poem, professional actors usually mark the text of a poem to indicate such things as which words to stress, where to pause and where to vary the pace of their reading. Marking a poem can help you to develop an effective reading. Here are the first lines of Yeats's poem 'An Irish Airman Foresees His Death' (see page 74). The poem is not divided into stanzas, but is a sequence of four-line sections held together by the rhyme scheme abab, cdcd, etc. The metre of each eight-syllable line is iambic, so if you mark the regular pattern of stresses the lines look like this:

× / × / × / × /
I know that I shall meet my fate

× / × / × / × /
Somewhere among the clouds above;

× / × / × / × /
Those that I fight I do not hate,

× / × / × / × /
Those that I guard I do not love.

Reading aloud notes

When interpreting a poem by reading it aloud, however, a speaker is likely to stress those syllables and words which emphasise its meaning, rather than merely sticking monotonously to the regular pattern.

Here is an example showing how a student marked these lines when preparing to read Yeats's poem aloud:

× ↗ × × × / / /
I know that I shall meet my fate

× × / × / × ↘
Somewhere among the clouds above; || Pause

/ × × × × × ↗
Those that I fight | I do not hate,

/ × × ↗ × × × ↘
Those that I guard | I do not love ...

Very even pace

Key to the markings used

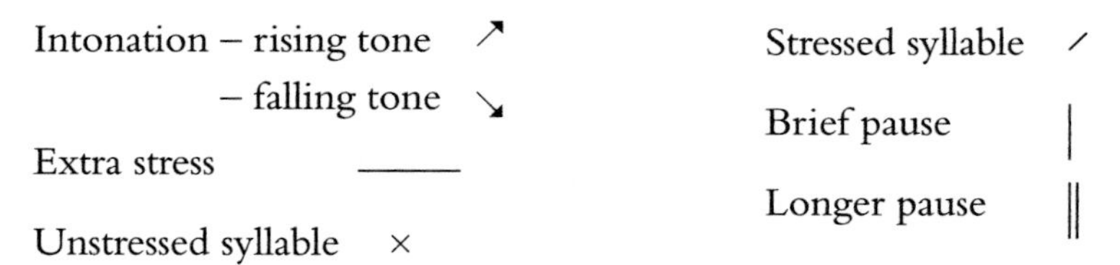

Relationships

I wish I could remember that first day

About the poet

Christina Rossetti (1830–94) was born and lived most of her life in London. She published her first volume of poetry at the age of 16. She was a devout Christian, and her poetry often reflects her religious beliefs. In general she deals with subjects such as lost love and happiness, acceptance, isolation and death.

About the poem

This poem comes from a sequence of love poems that were published in 1881. Christina Rossetti claimed that the poems were variations on Elizabeth Barrett Browning's sequence of love poems, 'Sonnets from the Portuguese' (see page 12), because they were the sort of poems that Elizabeth Barrett Browning might have written if she had been unhappy instead of happy.

The poem is a **sonnet**, a poem with 14 lines, each of which usually has 10 syllables and the same **iambic** pattern of **stressed** and unstressed syllables. Sonnets can have a variety of different **rhyme schemes**. The rhyme scheme can be described by giving each new **rhyme** the next letter of the alphabet. Thus, the complete rhyme scheme of this sonnet is abba abba cdd ccd. There are two main types of sonnet – the Petrarchan sonnet (see page 12) and the Shakespearian sonnet (see page 28).

In the poem, Christina Rossetti describes the feelings of a person who is unable to recall the day when she and her lover first met. She uses a **metaphor** in lines 7 and 8, suggesting that her feelings were buds on a tree that would blossom at a later date. A metaphor is a word (or words) which create a picture or **image** in the mind of the reader. The poet does this by comparing a person or object with something else in order to describe that person or object. For instance, you might describe an angry person by saying 'his eyes were on fire' or say that someone who was afraid 'was rooted to the ground with fear'. You do not mean that the first person's eyes are actually burning or that the second person has really grown roots. You are suggesting that the first person's eyes are bright with anger and that the second person is so frightened that they have become as unable to move as a tree or a plant.

Here are two other metaphors:

- A blanket of mist shrouded the trees.
- Pain gnawed at his leg.

I wish I could remember that first day

I wish I could remember that first day,
First hour, first moment of your meeting me,
If bright or dim the season, it might be
Summer or Winter for aught I can say;
So unrecorded did it slip away, 5
So blind was I to see and to foresee,
So dull to mark the budding of my tree
That would not blossom yet for many a May.
If only I could recollect it, such
A day of days! I let it come and go 10
As traceless as a thaw of bygone snow;
It seemed to mean so little, meant so much;
If only now I could recall that touch,
First touch of hand in hand – Did one but know!

CHRISTINA ROSSETTI
(1830–94)

4 *aught* – anything
7 *mark* – notice
11 *bygone* – past

Activities

Discussion and notemaking

Discuss these questions in pairs, each making notes of your ideas, then share them in either a group or class discussion.

1. Study the first four lines of the poem and discuss what the person in the poem is unable to recall about their first meeting.
2. What do lines 5–8 tell us about the reasons why the person is unable to recall their first meeting? Study the explanation of what a metaphor is (see above) and discuss the meaning of the image that Christina Rossetti uses in lines 7 and 8.
3. Which words and phrases in lines 9–13 show that the person regrets being unable to remember their first meeting?
4. What is the significance of the last four words of the poem? What do they tell you about how the person feels about that first day? Discuss what you think might have happened to make her feel this way and give reasons for your suggestions.

5. Study the list of suggested titles for the poem (below). Do you think any of them is suitable? Suggest other possible titles and then agree on one for the poem.

   - Missed opportunity
   - Lost love
   - The precious moment
   - That special day
   - Wistful recollections

Speaking and listening

❧ Look back at your notes and, in groups, discuss how to read the poem aloud so that it reflects the person's **mood**. Decide what the **tone** of the poem is, and choose someone to read the poem aloud to the rest of the class. Compare the different readings and decide whose reading most successfully conveyed the woman's mood.

Writing

❧ Write the diary entry that the person in the poem might have written if she had chosen to write down her thoughts in her diary rather than in a poem. Then, in pairs, compare your diary entries to check that you have not left out anything that is said in the poem. Decide which of your entries most accurately captures the thoughts and feelings expressed in the poem.

First Love

About the poet

John Clare (1793–1864) was born in a Northamptonshire village. As a youngster he was ashamed of his love of poetry, because he did not think it was a proper subject for a village labourer's child to be interested in. The writing of verse came easily and naturally to him, but he never learned how to punctuate or to spell uniformly. Although his first book of poetry was a success, he never made enough money from his later books to support himself and his family, and he became depressed and mentally ill. For the last 27 years of his life he was regarded as a lunatic, and he died in Northampton General Lunatic Asylum.

About the poem

This poem was written after Clare was taken into an asylum. In it he recalls his childhood friend, a farmer's daughter called Mary Joyce, who became his idealised love. She haunted his poetry and his fantasies throughout his life. Although unpunctuated, the poem is written in a regular pattern of verses, each of which has eight lines and the rhyme scheme ababcdcd.

First Love

I ne'er was struck before that hour
  With love so sudden and so sweet
Her face it bloomed like a sweet flower
  And stole my heart away complete
My face turned pale a deadly pale 5
  My legs refused to walk away
And when she looked what could I ail
  My life and all seemed turned to clay

And then my blood rushed to my face
  And took my eyesight quite away 10
The trees and bushes round the place
  Seemed midnight at noon day
I could not see a single thing
  Words from my eyes did start
They spake as chords do from the string 15
  And blood burnt round my heart

Are flowers the winters choice
  Is loves bed always snow
She seemed to hear my silent voice
  Not loves appeal to know 20
I never saw so sweet a face
  As that I stood before
My heart has left its dwelling place
  And can return no more

JOHN CLARE
(1793–1864)

7 *ail* – suffer 14 *start* – spring suddenly 15 *spake* – spoke

Activities

Writing

Although Clare did not punctuate this poem, modern editors often do so in order to help the reader to discover its meaning. Either make a copy of the poem or put it on the word-processor and then work with a partner to punctuate it. You will need to consider whether there are some places in the poem where you might use a semi-colon, rather than a full stop, a question mark or a comma. As you work on the punctuation, consider the questions in the Discussion and notemaking section (below). Each keep notes of your answers, so that you can refer to them when sharing your ideas.

Discussion and notemaking

Discuss these questions in pairs.

1. Which words and phrases in lines 1–12 tell you how the young man in the poem felt when he first fell in love?
2. How do lines 13–16 show the strength of his feeling? Which of the three images in these lines do you think is the most effective? Explain why.
3. What ideas about the nature of love are contained in lines 17 and 18? What do they suggest about the young man's feelings about love and his experience of it?
4. What does line 19 tell you about the young woman's reaction to how he looks at her?
5. What does line 20 tell you about how her response to him makes him feel?
6. How do the last four lines of the poem echo the first four lines of the poem? In your own words, explain what the last two lines tell you about the young man's feelings.
7. In groups, compare your punctuated versions of the poem and discuss the reasons for any differences.

How do I love thee?

About the poet

Elizabeth Barrett Browning (1806–61) was the eldest of 12 children. She was largely self-educated and published her first book of poems in 1820, when she was only 14. By 1845 she was an established poet. In that year she met Robert Browning, whom she married in secret against her father's will. They went to Italy, where they lived until her death.

About the poem

This poem is one of 44 love poems which were first published in 1850. The poems include those that were written in secret before she married Browning and ones that she wrote afterwards, and were given the title 'Sonnets from the Portuguese' because Browning had once called her 'his Portuguese'.

This sonnet is a Petrarchan sonnet. The name comes from the Italian poet Petrarch (1304–74), who was the first person to use this form. A Petrarchan sonnet is often divided into an eight-line section, known as the **octave**, followed by a six-line section, called the **sestet**. There is frequently a break in the thought or feeling between the two parts. The rhyme scheme of Petrarchan sonnets can vary, but in many of them only two rhymes are used in the octave and only two rhymes in the sestet. The rhyme scheme of a typical Petrarchan sonnet is abbaabba cdcdcd.

Sonnet 93

How do I love thee? Let me count the ways.
I love thee to the depth and breadth and height
My soul can reach, when feeling out of sight
For the ends of Being and ideal Grace.
I love thee to the level of every day's 5
Most quiet need, by sun and candle-light.
I love thee freely, as men strive for Right;
I love thee purely, as they turn from Praise.
I love thee with the passion put to use
In my old griefs, and with my childhood's faith. 10
I love thee with a love I seemed to lose
With my lost saints, – I love thee with the breath,
Smiles, tears, of all my life! – and, if God choose,
I shall but love thee better after death.

ELIZABETH BARRETT BROWNING
(1806–61)

Activities

Discussion and notemaking

Discuss these questions in groups, each making notes of your ideas, so that you can share them in a class discussion.

1. List the answers that the poet gives to the question asked in line 1.
2. Which of the answers that are given do you think most effectively shows the strength of the woman's love? Explain why.
3. Discuss how the poet uses references to the present (lines 2–8), the past (lines (10–12), and the future (lines 12–14) to express her total commitment.
4. Notice how most of the words in the poem have only one or two syllables. What effect does this have on the **pace** of the poem?
5. Discuss the poet's use of repetition. What effect is achieved by repeating the phrase 'I love thee' throughout the poem? How does the woman's final statement of her love vary from her other statements? What effect does this have?
6. Talk about these words and decide which one best sums up the mood of the poem.
   - sombre
   - joyful
   - passionate
   - resigned
   - devoted

Speaking and listening

❧ Imagine that you are producing a radio programme on love poetry which is to include this poem. Work with a partner and make a tape-recording in which one of you introduces the poem and the other reads it. Before you make your recording, look back at your notes, discuss what you want your reading to convey about the woman's thoughts and feelings and together draft an introduction to the poem. When you have made your recordings, play them to the rest of the class. Decide which of them has the best introduction and which has the best reading.

If thou must love me

About the poet

For details of Elizabeth Barrett Browning see page 12.

About the poem

This is another of the poems from 'Sonnets from the Portuguese'. The poet uses a variation of the Petrarchan sonnet (see page 12) to present an imagined speech addressed to her lover.

Sonnet 14

If thou must love me, let it be for nought
Except for love's sake only. Do not say
'I love her for her smile – her look – her way
Of speaking gently, – for a trick of thought
That falls in well with mine, and certes brought 5
A sense of pleasant ease on such a day' –
For these things in themselves, Belovèd, may
Be changed, or change for thee, – and love, so wrought,
May be unwrought so. Neither love me for
Thine own dear pity's wiping my cheeks dry, – 10
A creature might forget to weep, who bore
Thy comfort long, and lose thy love thereby!
But love me for love's sake, that evermore
Thou mayst love on, through love's eternity.

ELIZABETH BARRETT BROWNING
(1806–61)

4 *trick of thought* – the way you think
5 *certes* – certainly
8 *wrought* – made

Activities

Discussion and notemaking

Discuss these questions in pairs, each making notes of your ideas, then share them with another pair in a group discussion.

1. Trace the development of the woman's thoughts in this poem:

- What does she say to her lover in lines 1–2?
- Why does she not want him to love her just for her appearance and behaviour (lines 2–9)?
- Why does she not want him to love her out of pity (lines 9–12)?
- How does what she says in the final two lines echo what she says in the first two lines?

Speaking and listening

❧ In groups, experiment with different ways of reading the poem aloud and decide what kind of imagined speech the woman in the poem is making. Is it a) a plea? b) a statement? c) a demand? Then choose a spokesperson to explain your views to the rest of the class.

Writing

❧ Compare the thoughts about love which Elizabeth Barrett Browning expresses in this sonnet with the sonnet on page 12. Say which of the poems you think most effectively conveys her intensity of feelings and her ideas about the ideal kind of love.

❧ Express your own thoughts about the ideas which Elizabeth Barrett Browning explores in her two sonnets either in a **free-verse** poem or a short piece of prose.

The Passionate Shepherd to His Love

About the poet

Christopher Marlowe (1564–93) lived at the same time as William Shakespeare (see page 28). The son of a shoemaker, Marlowe was educated at the King's School Canterbury and Cambridge University. On leaving Cambridge, he quickly established a reputation as a playwright, with plays such as *Tamburlaine the Great* and *Dr Faustus*. But there were rumours that his religious and political opinions were treacherous, and the authorities began an investigation into his activities. Then, at the age of 29, he was stabbed to death at a Deptford tavern while in the company of two government spies.

About the poem

This poem was written while Marlowe was still at Cambridge University. The poem is both a **lyric** poem (see below) and an example of the type of **pastoral** poem that was popular during the reign of Queen Elizabeth I (1558–1603). A pastoral poem describes an imaginary world, in which shepherds and shepherdesses live an idealised life in a perfect countryside. Pastoral poems appealed to educated Elizabethans because they reflected the wish for a simple country life, away from the pressures of court and town, free of cares and dedicated to simple pleasures.

A lyric poem is a poem in which the poet's main purpose is to express personal thoughts and feelings. Many lyric poems, including this one, consist of verses which can be set to music and made into a song. In this poem Marlowe uses four-line verses or **quatrains**. Each quatrain has the rhyme scheme aabb, and many of the lines have eight syllables and a regular iambic **metre** consisting of an unstressed syllable followed by a stressed syllable.

The Passionate Shepherd to His Love

Come live with me and be my love,
And we will all the pleasures prove
That hills and valleys, dales and fields,
And all the craggy mountains yields.

There we will sit upon the rocks 5
And see the shepherds feed their flocks,
By shallow rivers to whose falls
Melodious birds sing madrigals.

And I will make thee beds of roses
And a thousand fragrant posies, 10
A cap of flowers, and a kirtle
Embroidered all with leaves of myrtle;

A gown made of the finest wool
Which from our pretty lambs we pull;
Fair linèd slippers for the cold, 15
With buckles of the purest gold;

A belt of straw and ivy buds,
With coral clasps and amber studs:
And if these pleasures may thee move,
Come live with me, and be my love. 20

The shepherds' swains shall dance and sing
For thy delight each May morning:
If these delights thy mind may move,
Then live with me and be my love.

CHRISTOPHER MARLOWE
(1564–93)

2 *prove* – experience
11 *kirtle* – gown
18 *coral* – hard, pink, rock-like substance, used in jewellery
18 *amber* – yellowish translucent resin, used in jewellery
19 *move* – influence, persuade
21 *swains* – country youths

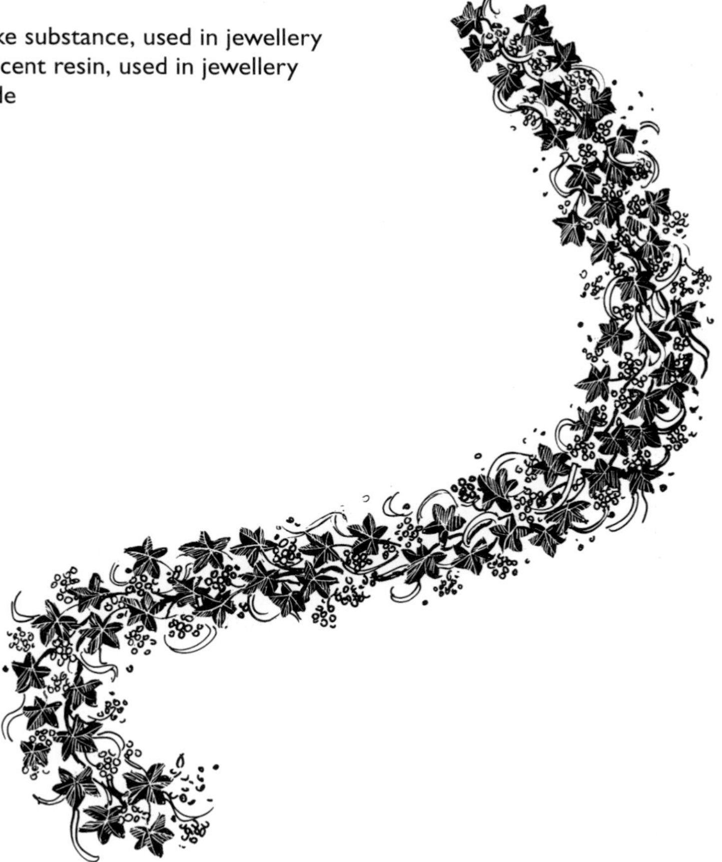

Activities

Discussion and notemaking

Discuss these questions in groups, each making notes of your ideas so that you can share them in a class discussion.

1. List the pleasures that the 'passionate shepherd' offers to the person he is addressing.
2. Discuss the use that Marlowe makes of the senses in describing these pleasures.
3. Discuss how the pleasures that the shepherd offers present an idealised picture of love rather than a realistic one.
4. Notice how in several lines Marlowe uses two words that start with the same letter. The use of several words starting with the same letter in order to create a particular effect is called **alliteration**. In which of the verses does Marlowe use a) alliteration b) repetition to help create an appropriate pastoral mood?
5. Talk about the following phrases and decide which one best sums up what the passionate shepherd is offering.
   - a life of comfort and pleasure
   - a life of wealth and ease
   - a life of sensuous delights
   - a life free from trouble and cares

Speaking and listening

❧ In pairs, discuss how in much of the poem Marlowe uses the regular iambic metre to develop a pace suggesting the pastoral scene which he is describing. Rehearse a reading of the poem which uses the poem's **rhythm** in order to create the effect you wish your reading to achieve. ❧ Then form groups and compare your readings. Discuss whose reading works best and why.

Writing and illustrating

❧ In pairs, discuss different ways of presenting this poem pictorially Then, on your own, produce either a poster, a picture strip or a collage to convey the ideas expressed in the poem. You could type the poem onto the computer and use a graphics package to help to develop your ideas.

The Nymph's Reply to the Shepherd

About the poet

Sir Walter Ralegh (*c.*1552 –1618) was born in Devon and educated at Oxford University. He was a soldier and explorer and early in his career was a favourite of Queen Elizabeth I, who knighted him in 1584. Later he fell out of favour, was accused of intrigue and spent many years living as a prisoner in the Tower of London. He was released to lead an expedition to South America in search of gold. However, the expedition was a failure and on his return Ralegh was executed. Many of Ralegh's poems have been lost, but those few that have survived show that he was a talented poet.

About the poem

In this poem, Ralegh mimics the verse form that Marlowe uses in 'The Passionate Shepherd to His Love' (see page 16–17) to present a reply to Marlowe's poem. He follows the pastoral tradition by saying that the nymph is replying to the shepherd, but he makes her words show the unreality of the shepherd's offer.

The Nymph's Reply to the Shepherd

If all the world and love were young,
And truth in every shepherd's tongue,
These pretty pleasures might me move
To live with thee and be thy love.

Time drives the flocks from field to fold 5
When rivers rage and rocks grow cold,
And Philomel becometh dumb;
The rest complains of cares to come.

The flowers do fade, and wanton fields
To wayward winter reckoning yields; 10
A honey tongue, a heart of gall,
In fancy's spring, but sorrow's fall.

Thy gowns, thy shoes, thy bed of roses,
Thy cap, thy kirtle, and thy posies
Soon break, soon wither, soon forgotten – 15
In folly ripe, in reason rotten.

Thy belt of straw and ivy buds,
Thy coral clasps and amber studs,
All these in me no means can move
To come to thee and be thy love. 20

But could youth last and love still breed,
Had joys no date nor age no need,
Then these delights my mind might move
To live with thee and be thy love.

Sir Walter Ralegh
(*c.*1552–1618)

3 *move* – persuade
7 *Philomel* – nightingale
9 *wanton* – luxuriant
10 *reckoning yields* – gives way to
11 *gall* – bitterness
12 *fancy's* – day-dream's
12 *spring* – (1) starting up (2) the season
12 *fall* – (1) decline (2) autumn (as in the American 'Fall')
14 *kirtle* – gown
18 *stud* – button
22 *date* – ending

Activities

Discussion and notemaking

Discuss these questions in groups, make notes, and then share your ideas in a class discussion.

1. What does the nymph say in the first verse which explains why she does not respond to the shepherd's offer?
2. List the reasons the nymph gives in lines 5–20 for rejecting the appeal of the imaginary world and idealised life which the shepherd offers.
3. Discuss how verses 2–5 in Ralegh's poem echo and contrast with verses 2–5 in Marlowe's poem. Which words and phrases in the nymph's reply most effectively reveal the unreality of the world the shepherd describes?
4. After discussing the last verse, say why the nymph finally rejects both the shepherd and his world. What is the tone of this verse?

Speaking and listening

❧ Work with a partner and practise reading Ralegh's poem to each other, finding effective ways to convey the nymph's rejection of the shepherd's offer.

❧ In groups, experiment with ways of presenting readings of Marlowe's poem and Ralegh's poem together in order to bring out the contrast between the shepherd's offer and the nymph's reply. Think about how you might show that Ralegh's poem echoes Marlowe's poem, and experiment with different voices and different ways of breaking up and interweaving the two poems.

Writing

❧ Explain how Marlowe presents a picture of idealised love in his poem 'The Passionate Shepherd to His Love' and how Ralegh in 'The Nymph's Reply to the Shepherd' shows that such a view is unrealistic.

❧ A number of poets have made fun of the attitude of Marlowe's shepherd by writing a **parody** of his poem. A parody is a piece of writing which mimics the **style** of another writer to ridicule its characteristic features. Either on your own or with a partner write a contemporary parody of Marlowe's poem. Before you begin, use the library to find the parody of Marlowe's poem written by John Donne entitled 'The Baite' and one by Cecil Day Lewis which uses Marlowe's first line as its title.

To My Dear and Loving Husband

About the poet

Anne Bradstreet (*c.*1612–72) wrote the first book of poems by a woman to be published in America. Born in England, she married Simon Bradstreet, a young Puritan parson, in 1628 and two years later they emigrated to America. They helped to found the colony at Massachusetts Bay in New England. In spite of the hardships of colonial life and the demands of being the mother of eight children, she wrote continually in 'time stolen from sleep'. Her poems were observations of nature, of daily life and of her religious experience.

About the poem

This is an autobiographical poem addressed to her husband in the way that a letter might have been written to him. The poem is written in rhyming **couplets**, pairs of lines which rhyme. Each of the lines has ten syllables and is an iambic **pentameter**.

To My Dear and Loving Husband

If ever two were one, then surely we.
If ever man were lov'd by wife, then thee;
If ever wife was happy in a man,
Compare with me ye women if you can.
I prize thy love more then whole Mines of gold, 5
Or all the riches that the East doth hold.
My love is such that Riches cannot quench,
Nor ought but love from thee, give recompense.
Thy love is such I can no way repay.
The heavens reward thee manifold I pray. 10
Then while we live, in love let's so persever,
That when we live no more, we may live ever.

ANNE BRADSTREET
(*c.*1612–72)

2 *then* – than
6 *riches* – valuable possessions, i.e. pearls
6 *East doth hold* – East Asia contains
7 *quench* – cool
8 *ought* – anything
10 *manifold* – many times over
11 *persever* – continue steadfastly

Activities

Discussion and notemaking

In pairs, discuss these questions. Note down your answers, then share your views in a group discussion.

1. Write down the words and phrases in the poem which express the depth of the wife's love for her husband. Which of the images that she uses in lines 5–7 do you think is the most effective? Explain why.
2. Which lines show that her husband loves her equally strongly?
3. In the final four lines, what evidence is there of the wife's religious faith?
4. How would you describe the tone of the poem? Which of these words do you think most accurately describes it?
   - sentimental
   - joyful
   - affectionate
   - devoted
   - passionate
   - tender
   - detached
   - emotional
   - ecstatic

   Can you suggest any other(s)? Give your reasons.

Speaking and listening

❧ Role play a scene in which two people discuss what sort of wife and mother they think the person in the poem must be and the impression they have formed of her from reading the poem. Show your role plays to the rest of the class and discuss the picture of the woman which they present.

Writing

❧ Try writing a similar poem to Anne Bradstreet's in which you use rhyming couplets. Either write a reply 'To My Dear and Loving Wife' or write a poem 'To My Cold and Wayward Husband/Wife'.

A Woman to Her Lover

About the poet

All that is known about Christina Walsh is that she was born in 1750 and died in about 1800. In her later years, therefore, she could have been aware of the new ideas spreading across Europe at the time of the French Revolution (1789). She may also have been familiar with the writings of Mary Wollstonecraft (1759–97), particularly *A Vindication of the Rights of Women* (1792). 'A Woman to Her Lover' confidently assumes the equality of women with men and their equal rights within marriage.

About the poem

The form of 'A Woman to Her Lover' is unusual for the late eighteenth century. It is written in free verse, its uneven lines arranged in **stanzas** of different lengths. Each stanza is centred around a single idea, to make a **verse paragraph** like a paragraph in prose.

A Woman to Her Lover

Do you come to me to bend me to your will
As conqueror to the vanquished,
To make of me a bondslave,
To bear you children, wearing out my life
In drudgery and silence? 5
No servant will I be.
If that be what you ask, O Lover I refuse you!

Or if you think to wed with one from heaven sent
Whose every deed and word and wish is golden,
A wingless angel who can do no wrong, 10
Go! – I am no doll to dress and sit for feeble worship.
If that be what you ask, fool, I refuse you!

Or if you think in me to find
A creature who will have no greater joy
Than gratify your clamorous desire, 15
My skin soft only for your fond caresses,
My body supple only for your sense delight,
Oh shame, and pity and abasement.
Not for you the hand of any wakened woman of our time.

But Lover, if you ask of me 20
That I shall be your comrade, friend, and mate,
To live and work, to love and die with you,
That so together we may know the purity and height
Of passion, and of joy and sorrow,
Then O husband, I am yours forever. 25
And our co-equal love will make the stars to laugh with joy
And we shall have the music of the spheres for bridal march
And to its circling fugue pass on, hand holding hand
Until we reach the very heart of God.

CHRISTINA WALSH
(1750–?1800)

15 *clamorous* – demanding
18 *abasement* – humiliation
27 *music of the spheres* – perfect harmonies supposedly of heavenly bodies
28 *fugue* – musical composition in which several parts enter in sequence

Activities

Discussion and notemaking

On your own, make notes in answer to the following questions. Then share your ideas in a group discussion, and finally compare the group's ideas in a class discussion.

1. In the first three stanzas of the poem the woman describes three male attitudes to women which she rejects. Pick the line from each stanza which you think best sums up the attitude she is rejecting, and write one sentence on each stanza to summarise what it says.
2. In the final stanza the woman states how she wishes her lover to regard her and treat her. Make a list of the attitudes and behaviour she expects of him. What does she say will be the result of him treating her in this way?

Speaking and listening

❧ Imagine that Anne Bradstreet's poem 'To My Dear and Loving Husband' and Christina Walsh's poem 'A Woman to Her Lover' are to be read in front of a television audience, who have been invited to discuss their responses to them in a televised debate. Choose two people to read the poems and another person to act as the television presenter, then role play the debate.

Writing

❧ Write 'A Man's Reply to His Lover' in a similar style, in which the writer either agrees to behave in the way that the woman in Christina Walsh's poem expects, or in which the man states what attitudes towards him he expects his lover to have if she wishes to become his wife.
❧ Compare the view expressed by Anne Bradstreet in her poem 'To My Dear and Loving Husband' with the view expressed by Christina Walsh in her poem 'A Woman to Her Lover'. Comment on the style and language of the poems, and their different forms.

Love and Friendship

About the poet

Emily Brontë (1818–48) and her sisters, Charlotte and Anne, lived in the isolated village of Haworth in Yorkshire, where their father was the vicar. As children, Emily and Anne began to write stories and poems set in an imaginary kingdom called Gondal. Emily is most famous for her novel *Wuthering Heights*, but her literary reputation was not established until after her death. Only a few of her poems were published in her lifetime and a joint volume of poetry, which she and her sisters published under the pen-names of Currer, Acton and Ellis Bell, sold only two copies.

About the poem

In this poem Emily Brontë uses two comparisons to express her thoughts about love and friendship. She says that 'Love is like the wild rose briar' while friendship is 'like the holly tree.' A comparison which is made using 'like' or 'as' is called a **simile**. Here are some examples of similes which are used in the Bible:

- All we like sheep have gone astray.
- Be ye therefore wise as serpents, and harmless as doves.
- He maketh the deep to boil like a pot.

Love and Friendship

Love is like the wild rose briar,
Friendship like the holly tree.
The holly is dark when the rose briar blooms,
But which will bloom most constantly?

The wild rose briar is sweet in spring, 5
Its summer blossoms scent the air;
Yet wait till winter comes again
And who will call the wild-briar fair?

Then scorn the silly rose-wreath now,
And deck thee with the holly's sheen, 10
That when December blights thy brow
He still may leave thy garland green.

EMILY JANE BRONTË
(1818–48)

9 *silly* – ridiculous
10 *deck* – decorate
11 *blights* – spoils
11 *brow* – forehead

Activities

Discussion and notemaking

Discuss these questions in pairs, each making notes of your ideas, then share them in a group discussion.

1. Read the poem on your own and write down one or two sentences summing up what you think Emily Brontë is saying about love and friendship in this poem. Then compare your ideas with those of your partner.
2. Discuss the simile Emily Brontë uses to describe love. List the ways in which love is like a wild rose briar. What impression of love does she give by this comparison?
3. List the ways in which she says friendship is like a holly tree. What impression does this comparison give of friendship?
4. How does the poet sum up her thoughts in the final verse? What is her message to the reader? Pick out the key words and phrases she uses in this verse to convey the contrast she feels between love and friendship. Discuss the use she makes of alliteration in lines 11 and 12.

Speaking and listening

❧ 'Love offers more than friendship, but friendship is likely to last longer than love.' Discuss this statement in a class debate about love and friendship. Before you begin, look back at your notes on the poem and, in the debate, refer to the ideas Emily Brontë expresses and say whether or not you agree with them.

Writing

❧ 'Love and Friendship' is written in four-line verses with the rhyme scheme abcb. Try to write one or two similar verses of your own expressing your ideas about love and friendship. Before you begin, study the two attempts below and discuss them with your partner. Which of the two verses do you think is most successful in conveying the writer's ideas – Joanne's verse or Derek's?

Friendship like the tall oak's trunk
Survives the winter long.
Love's leaves in autumn wither and curl.
Its ties are not so strong.

Joanne

Friendship's solid as a stone.
Love is like a raging fire.
Friendship's warm like a scarf
But love is hot with desire.

Derek

Let me not to the marriage of true minds

About the poet

William Shakespeare (1564–1616) was born in Stratford-upon-Avon, where he grew up and was married. He then moved to London. By 1592, he was established as an actor and playwright, working for the leading company, the Lord Chamberlain's Men, which built its own playhouse, The Globe, in 1598. He became England's most famous playwright, writing 37 plays including *Hamlet*, *Julius Caesar*, *Macbeth* and *Romeo and Juliet*. In addition to his plays, Shakespeare wrote a sequence of 154 sonnets about different experiences of love.

About the poem

All of Shakespeare's sonnets have the same pattern. The first 12 lines consist of three 4-line sections, known as quatrains, in which alternate lines rhyme. The sonnet ends with two lines which rhyme, known as a rhyming couplet. The rhyme scheme of a Shakespeare sonnet is, therefore, abba cdcd efef gg. This pattern has become known as the Shakespearian sonnet.

The thoughts and feelings which Shakespeare expresses in his sonnets are probably fictional rather than autobiographical. 'Sonnet 116' declares the belief that no obstacle can get in the way of true love.

In this poem Shakespeare writes about both Love and Time as if they are people. In line 9, he says that Love is not a fool or jester, and he writes about Time as if he is an old man wielding a sickle and carrying an hour-glass. Describing either something abstract, such as love and time, or an animal or object as though it is a person, is called **personification**. Often, to indicate that personification is being used, the first letter of whatever is being described is given a capital in the way that Time is given a capital in line 9.

Sonnet 116

Let me not to the marriage of true minds
Admit impediments: love is not love
Which alters when it alteration finds,
Or bends with the remover to remove.
O no, it is an ever fixèd mark 5
That looks on tempests and is never shaken;
It is the star to every wand'ring bark,
Whose worth's unknown, although his height be taken.
Love's not Time's fool, though rosy lips and cheeks
Within his bending sickle's compass come; 10
Love alters not with his brief hours and weeks,
But bears it out even to the edge of doom.
 If this be error and upon me prov'd,
 I never writ, nor no man ever lov'd.

William Shakespeare
(1564–1616)

1 *Let me not* – May I never
1 *true* – faithful
2 *Admit impediments* – accept obstacles
4 *Or bends ... remove* – withdraws when the other's love does
5 *mark* – buoy
7 *bark* – ship
8 *his* – its
8 *height* – altitude (used for navigation)
9 *Love's not Time's fool* – true love isn't ruled by time
10 *compass* – reach
12 *edge of doom* – brink of Judgement Day

Activities

Discussion and notemaking

Discuss the following questions in pairs, each making notes of your ideas, then in a group compare your notes with other people's.

1. Study the first 12 lines of the poem. Discuss how Shakespeare makes a statement in the first and second lines, then uses lines 2–12 to give examples which support his viewpoint. Find three quotations which describe true love and three quotations which describe love that is not true love. List them in two columns under the headings 'true love' and 'not true love', and rewrite each of them in your own words.

2. Study the final rhyming couplet. What does Shakespeare say in these two lines to try to convince the reader that his view of true love is right?

3. Discuss the metaphors Shakespeare uses in lines 5–6 and 7–8 and how he uses personification in lines 9–12. Which of his images do you find most effective? Explain why.

Speaking and listening

❧ Either copy out the poem on lined paper, leaving a space between each line, or type it onto a word-processor using double spacing between the lines. Think about how you would prepare a reading of the poem in order to put across the person's conviction that his views are right, bring out his growing confidence, and make the final couplet a strong conclusion. Mark the words which you are going to stress, and places where you intend to pause or to vary the volume or pace of your reading. Then compare your marked scripts in a group discussion, practise reading the poem in different ways, and decide whose marked instructions are most effective.

Writing

❧ Imagine you are a feature writer for a magazine for teenagers. Write a short article 'How to tell if it's true love' in which you explain what Shakespeare had to say on the subject.
❧ Compare what Shakespeare says about love in 'Sonnet 116' with what Emily Brontë says in her poem 'Love and Friendship' on page 26. Comment on the structure of the two poems and the language and **imagery** the poets use to express their ideas.

When we two parted

About the poet

George Gordon, Lord Byron (1788–1824) had an unhappy early childhood. His father died when Byron was 3, his mother was violent, and he had a drunken nurse. Because he had a club foot, he was determined to succeed at games. He went to Cambridge University and his first book of poems was published while he was still a student. For a time in his twenties he was a popular figure in London society, renowned for his good looks, his poetry and his outrageous behaviour. However, in 1816, the scandal resulting from his private life forced him to leave England for ever. He settled in Italy, where he became friends with Shelley (see page 118). He was an ardent supporter of the Greeks in their attempt to win independence from Turkey, but died of fever at the age of 36 while helping to assemble forces for the struggle.

About the poem

This lyric poem describes the feelings of a person when they hear news of a former lover several years after a secret relationship. Byron was inspired to write sentimental love poetry to Lady Frances Webster, whom he idealised. This poem was written in 1816 when he learned that, far from being an innocent young woman, she had been scandalously involved with the Duke of Wellington. While these facts provide an insight into how Byron came to write the poem, they do not mean that it must be interpreted historically. The poem is written in eight-line stanzas with the rhyme scheme ababcdcd.

When we two parted

When we two parted
In silence and tears,
Half broken-hearted
To sever for years,
Pale grew thy cheek and cold, 5
Colder thy kiss;
Truly that hour foretold
Sorrow to this.

The dew of the morning
Sunk chill on my brow – 10
It felt like the warning
Of what I feel now.
Thy vows are all broken,
And light is thy fame:
I hear thy name spoken, 15
And share in its shame.

They name thee before me,
A knell to mine ear;
A shudder comes o'er me –
Why wert thou so dear? 20
Thy know not I knew thee,
Who knew thee too well:–
Long, long shall I rue thee,
Too deeply to tell.

In secret we met – 25
In silence I grieve,
That thy heart could forget,
Thy spirit deceive.
If I should meet thee
After long years, 30
How should I greet thee?
With silence and tears.

George Gordon, Lord Byron
(1788–1824)

14 *light* – worthless
14 *fame* – reputation
18 *knell* – ominous sound
23 *rue* – miss

Activities

Discussion and notemaking

Discuss these questions in pairs, each making notes of your ideas, then share them in a class discussion.

1. What do the first 12 lines tell you about the parting and how the person in the poem felt about it at the time? Pick out the words and phrases which describe the person's feelings. Why are these feelings described as a 'warning' (line 11)?
2. Discuss lines 13–16. What has the person learned about her/his former lover? How is she/he affected by the news?
3. Discuss verse 3. How does the person feel when other people talk about the former lover? Which words and phrases tell you how she/he feels? Discuss why she/he does not reveal that they knew one another.
4. In verse 4, the person reflects on how she/he feels now. Talk about how her/his feelings have changed (lines 25–28) yet still echo the feelings she/he felt when they parted (lines 29–32).
5. Suggest a title for the poem and give reasons for your choice.

Speaking and listening

❧ Imagine that instead of putting her/his thoughts and feelings into a poem, the person in the poem decided to talk confidentially to a trustworthy friend. Role play the scene in which she/he talks talk openly about her/his feelings. Before you begin, re-read the poem and look through your notes to help you to decide what the person would say.

❧ Prepare a reading of the poem. Think carefully about how you could use your voice, varying its volume and tone and altering the pace of your reading to bring out the depth of the character's feelings. Make a copy of the poem and mark the words that you are going to stress, places where you intend to speak more loudly or more softly, and where you intend to pause or alter the speed of your reading.

Writing

❧ Imagine that the person in the poem is sent a secret message by her/his former lover requesting a meeting. Write the letter she/he sends as a reply.

Since there's no help, come let us kiss and part

About the poet

Michael Drayton (1563–1631) was a contemporary of William Shakespeare (see page 28). He wrote a great deal, writing plays as well as poetry of all kinds. In addition to his sonnets, he wrote a historical **epic** *The Barons' Wars*, and a 30,000-line celebration of all the counties of England and Wales.

About the poem

This poem comes from a sequence of sonnets, 'Idea's Mirror', which Drayton wrote in 1594, inspired by his love for Anne Goodere. She married Sir Henry Rainsford, but she remained the object of Drayton's affection throughout his life; he himself never married. The poem is a Shakespearian sonnet (see page 28) which takes the form of a **dramatic monologue** (see page 95) in which a man addresses the woman he loves.

Before reading the poem, remind yourself what personification is (see page 28).

Sonnet 61

Since there's no help, come let us kiss and part;
  Nay, I have done, you get no more of me,
And I am glad, yea, glad with all my heart,
  That thus so cleanly I myself can free;
Shake hands for ever, cancel all our vows, 5
  And when we meet at any time again,
Be it not seen in either of our brows
  That we one jot of former love retain.
Now at the last gasp of Love's latest breath,
  When, his pulse failing, Passion speechless lies, 10
When Faith is kneeling by his bed of death,
  And Innocence is closing up his eyes;
    Now if thou wouldst, when all have given him over,
    From death to life thou mightst him yet recover.

MICHAEL DRAYTON
(1563–1631)

7 *brows* – expressions
8 *jot* – very small amount

Activities

Discussion and notemaking

Discuss these questions in pairs, each making notes of your ideas, then share them in either a group or class discussion.

1. Talk about the first eight lines of the poem. What does the person say? How does he feel? What do you think the woman he is addressing feels? At what stage in their relationship do you imagine him making this speech?
2. Which of the words listed below most accurately describes the mood that the speaker suggests he is feeling? Give reasons for your answer.
   - relief
   - acceptance
   - rejection
   - hopelessness
   - resignation
3. What scene is described in lines 9–12? What effect does the speaker hope this description will have on the person he adores?
4. Talk about how Drayton uses personification in lines 9–12 to help him to describe the scene, and to convey the person's emotions in an attempt to arouse his lover's sympathy.
5. What do the last two lines tell you about the person's real feelings?
6. Which of the phrases listed below best describes what the person in the poem is trying to do? Give reasons for your answer.
   - To express his regret at the ending of their relationship.
   - To persuade the person he loves to change her mind about ending their relationship.
   - To show that he no longer cares now that their relationship is over.
   - To convey the depth of his feelings and show how much he still wants the person to be his lover.

Speaking and listening

❧ Work with a partner. What do you think the woman whom the person is addressing is thinking and feeling? How will she respond to what he says? Role play a scene in which she tells a friend how she feels. Before you begin, re-read the poem and look back at your notes to remind yourself what the person in the poem says.

Writing

❧ Write a sonnet in reply to what is said in the poem, expressing the woman's response, saying how she feels about what her lover says.

Porphyria's Lover

About the poet

Robert Browning (1812–89) was the son of a bank clerk. He lived with his parents at Camberwell until, at the age of 34, he ran away with and married Elizabeth Barrett (see page 12). He had already published several books of poetry but they had not been financially successful, and at that time Elizabeth Barrett's poetry was more widely known. They went to live in Italy, and when another book of his poetry achieved only moderate success Browning became disheartened and for a number of years wrote very little. However, after he returned to London, following his wife's death in 1861, his earlier books were re-published and he achieved both fame and financial success, as one of the leading **Victorian** poets.

About the poem

This poem was first published under the title 'Madhouse Cells'. It takes the form of a dramatic monologue (see page 95), as if it were spoken by Porphyria's lover. He describes the events leading to Porphyria's death.

Porphyria's Lover

The rain set early in to-night,
  The sullen wind was soon awake,
It tore the elm-tops down for spite,
  And did its worst to vex the lake:
  I listened with heart fit to break. 5
When glided in Porphyria; straight
  She shut the cold out and the storm,
And kneeled and made the cheerless grate
  Blaze up, and all the cottage warm;
  Which done, she rose, and from her form 10
Withdrew the dripping cloak and shawl,
  And laid her soiled gloves by, untied
Her hat and let the damp hair fall,
  And, last, she sat down by my side
  And called me. When no voice replied, 15
She put my arm about her waist,
  And made her smooth white shoulder bare,
And all her yellow hair displaced,
  And, stooping, made my cheek lie there,
  And spread, o'er all, her yellow hair, 20
Murmuring how she loved me – she
  Too weak, for all her heart's endeavour,
To set its struggling passion free
  From pride, and vainer ties dissever,
  And give herself to me for ever: 25
But passion sometimes would prevail,
  Nor could to-night's gay feast restrain
A sudden thought of one so pale
  For love of her, and all in vain;
  So, she was come through wind and rain. 30
Be sure I looked up at her eyes
  Happy and proud; at last I knew
Porphyria worshipped me; surprise
  Made my heart swell, and still it grew
  While I debated what to do. 35
That moment she was mine, mine, fair,
  Perfectly pure and good: I found
A thing to do, and all her hair
  In one long yellow string I wound
  Three times her little throat around, 40

And strangled her. No pain felt she;
  I am quite sure she felt no pain.
As a shut bud that holds a bee,
  I warily oped her lids; again
  Laughed the blue eyes without a stain. 45
And I untightened next the tress
  About her neck; her cheek once more
Blushed bright beneath my burning kiss:
  I propped her head up as before,
  Only, this time *my* shoulder bore 50
Her head, which droops upon it still:
  The smiling rosy little head,
So glad it has its utmost will,
  That all it scorned at once is fled,
  And I, its love, am gained instead! 55
Porphyria's love: she guessed not how
  Her darling one wish would be heard.
And thus we sit together now,
  And all night long we have not stirred,
  And yet God has not said a word! 60

ROBERT BROWNING
(1812–89)

4 *vex* – make rough
6 *straight* – straight away
18 *displaced* – loosened
22 *endeavour* – attempts
24 *dissever* – cut
26 *prevail* – win
44 *oped* – opened
50 *bore* – supported
54 *scorned* – rejected
54 *fled* – gone

Activities

Discussion and notemaking

Begin by reading the poem through two or three times on your own, then write a few sentences or short phrases saying how you felt as you read it and what your first impressions are of Porphyria and of her lover. Discuss your responses with a partner and point out the lines in the poem which helped to give you those impressions. Then study the poem together, each making notes in answer to the following questions.

1. Talk about Porphyria and her reason for coming to see her lover. Why has she come? What do lines 15–21 and 31–33 tell you about her feelings? What do lines 26–29 tell you about where she has come from and what prompted her to come?

2. Talk about Porphyria's lover and his mixed feelings about her.

   - How did he feel before Porphyria arrives (line 5)?
   - Why was he unresponsive to her arrival and to her advances?
   - What do lines 21– 25 tell you about what he thought about her feelings towards him?
   - What do lines 28–29 tell you about his feelings?
   - What did he suddenly realise about her feelings (lines 31–34) and how did it make him feel?

3. Discuss what Porphyria's lover was thinking as he debated what to do (line 35). Why did he kill her? What do lines 36–37 and 52–58 tell you about his motives for killing her?

4. How does he feel after he has killed her? Which of the words below most accurately describe his feelings after he has killed her? Can you suggest any others?

   - remorse
   - elation
   - guilt
   - pain
   - fear
   - relief
   - satisfaction
   - fulfilment
   - justification
   - rapture

Speaking and listening

❧ Work in pairs and improvise a scene in which a police officer asks Porphyria's lover to explain why he killed her. Together draft the statement that Porphyria's lover might have signed. Then form groups and discuss the statements you have written.

❧ On your own, write the report that a psychiatrist might have written after reading the statement and interviewing Porphyria's lover. In groups, read and discuss the reports which each of you wrote.

Writing

❧ Imagine that, before setting out through the storm to visit her lover, Porphyria wrote an entry in her diary describing her feelings and her reasons for going. Write the entry in her diary.

❧ In pairs, produce a film script giving full details of how you would make a short film based on the poem.

❧ One critic has suggested that the main interest of the poem lies not in its story but in the two lovers' motives. Do you agree?

The Banks o' Doon

About the poet

Robert Burns (1759–96) is Scotland's most famous poet. He was born in Ayrshire and started to write poetry at the age of 15. He was educated by his father, and for much of his life worked on the land until his farm failed and he became an exciseman. He was offered a post on a plantation in Jamaica, but, when his early poems were a success in 1786, he moved for a time to Edinburgh, where his natural charm made him very popular. Two years later he returned to Ayrshire and married one of his many loves. Much of his writing was done against a background of hard physical labour and, later, increasingly poor health. He had a great interest in traditional Scottish songs and airs. 'I want to be more than ordinary *in song*,' he wrote. He contributed over 200 original or adapted songs to several books of songs and **ballads**.

About the poem

This poem is a lyric in which the poet describes the feelings of someone whose lover has proved false. There are two different versions of it, as Burns later adapted his original lyric to be sung to a traditional tune. 'Unless I be pleased with the tune,' Burns wrote, 'I can never make verses to it.'

The first version of the poem is written in four-line verses in which lines 2 and 4 rhyme, lines 1 and 3 have eight syllables and lines 2 and 4 have six syllables. In the second version, there are an extra two syllables in lines 2 and 4 in each verse so that the lyric fits a traditional tune.

Burns wrote his poems in a Scottish **dialect**. Note that in the pronunciation of the dialect, 'bough' in line 6 of the first version of the poem rhymes with 'true' in line 8 and 'thorn' in line 6 of the second version rhymes with 'return' in line 8.

The River Doon is a river which flows from the Ayrshire hills to Alloway near the west coast of Scotland.

(*First version*)

The Banks o' Doon

Ye flowery banks o' bonnie Doon,
   How can ye blume sae fair?
How can ye chant, ye little birds,
   And I sae fu' o' care!

Thou'll break my heart, thou bonnie bird 5
   That sings upon the bough;
Thou minds me o' the happy days
   When my fause Luve was true.

Thou'll break my heart, thou bonnie bird
   That sings beside thy mate; 10
For sae I sat, and sae I sang,
   And wist na o' my fate.

Aft hae I roved by bonnie Doon
  To see the woodbine twine,
And ilka bird sang o' its love; 15
  And sae did I o' mine.

Wi' lightsome heart I pu'd a rose,
  Frae aff its thorny tree;
And my fause Luver staw the rose,
  But left the thorn wi' me. 20

ROBERT BURNS
(1759–96)

2 *blume* – bloom
2 *sae* – so
4 *fu'* – full
7 *minds* – reminds
8 *fause* – unfaithful
12 *wist na* – knew not
13 *Aft hae* – often have
15 *ilka* – each
17 *pu'd* – plucked
18 *Frae aff* – from off
19 *staw* – stole

(*Second version*)

The Banks o' Doon

Ye banks and braes o' bonnie Doon,
  How can ye bloom sae fresh and fair?
How can ye chant, ye little birds,
  And I sae weary fu' o' care?
Thou'lt break my heart, thou warbling bird, 5
  That wantons thro' the flowering thorn:
Thou minds me o' departed joys,
  Departed never to return.

Aft hae I roved by bonnie Doon,
  To see the rose and woodbine twine; 10
And ilka bird sang o' its love,
  And fondly sae I did o' mine.
Wi' lightsome heart I pu'd a rose,
  Fu' sweet upon its thorny tree;
And my fause lover stole my rose, 15
  But ah! he left the thorn wi' me.

ROBERT BURNS
(1759–96)

1 *braes* – hillsides
2 *sae* – so
4 *fu'* – full
6 *wantons* – flits
7 *minds* – reminds
9 *Aft hae* – often have
11 *ilka* – each
13 *pu'd* – plucked
15 *fause* – unfaithful

Activities

Discussion and notemaking

On your own, study the first version of the poem and make notes in answer to the questions. Then share your ideas, first with a partner and afterwards in a class discussion.

1. What picture do you get of the riverside as you read this poem? Pick out the words and phrases which suggest this picture to you.

2. What effect do a) the sight of the flowers b) the singing of the bird have on the person in the poem? Why is the person so affected by them?

3. What do the rose and the thorn stand for in verse 5? What do verses 4 and 5 tell you about how the person used to feel during their riverside walks and how they feel now?

4. How would you describe the mood of the person in the poem? Which word(s) from the list below best fits the person's mood? Suggest other suitable words of your own.

   - sad
   - angry
   - dejected
   - resigned
   - hopeless
   - melancholic
   - solemn
   - wistful

Now read the second version of the poem and discuss these questions in pairs. Each make notes of your ideas, and then share them in a class discussion.

1. Which lines are different in the second version? Identify a) lines in which words have been added, and b) lines in which words and phrases have been changed completely.

2. Discuss the effects of the changes. Where Burns has included extra syllables to make the lines fit the tune of the song, do you think he has managed to add anything extra to the poem? Pick one line where you think the change adds something to the poem and one line where you think it does not add anything.

3. Compare lines 7 and 8 of the second version with lines 7–12 of the first version. Discuss the differences between the ideas expressed in these lines and the **language** used to express them. Which lines do you prefer? Explain why.

4. What does the final line of the second version tell you that you are not told in the first version? Is there any evidence in the first version to suggest whether the person is a man or a woman? Which of the two final lines do you find more effective – the shorter line or the longer line?

Speaking and listening

❧ *Either* find a copy of the traditional tune for which the second version of the poem was written, and then in groups present a performance or make a tape-recording of it *or* work with a partner, choose some suitable music to provide a background to a reading of the poem, rehearse it and then make a tape-recording of your reading.

Writing

❧ Compare the two different versions of the poem. Comment on the similarities and differences and say which of the two you think most effectively describes the thoughts and feelings of the jilted lover. Use the notes you made during the discussions to help you to plan your answer.

His being was in her alone

About the poet

Sir Philip Sidney (1554–86) was a famous member of the court of Queen Elizabeth 1 (1558–1603), renowned as a man of action and a man of learning. He went on several diplomatic missions, became a Member of Parliament, and was knighted in 1582. Four years later he was fatally wounded while serving in the Low Countries (the Netherlands, Belgium and Luxembourg) as Governor of Flushing. His body was brought back to England and he was buried in St Paul's Cathedral. He wrote both prose and poetry, little of which was published in his lifetime, although the manuscripts were widely circulated.

About the poem

This poem is like an **epitaph** (see page 59) commemorating the depth of love that two people felt for each other. The poem is written in rhyming couplets and arranged in such a way that the first pair of lines and the final pair of lines act as frames for the four-line verse in the middle of the poem.

His being was in her alone

His being was in her alone:
And he not being, she was none.

They joyed one joy, one grief they grieved;
One love they loved, one life they lived.
The hand was one, one was the sword, 5
That did his death, her death afford.

As all the rest, so now the stone
That tombs the two is justly one.

Sir Philip Sidney
(1554–86)

6 *afford* – cause
8 *tombs* – entombs

Activities

Discussion and notemaking

On your own, read the poem and write answers to the following questions. Then form groups and compare your answers in a group discussion.

1. What do you learn about the relationship between the man and the woman from the first two lines of the poem?
2. How do lines 3 and 4 reinforce what is said about the relationship in the first two lines?
3. What do lines 5 and 6 tell you about how the man and the woman died? How do you think the man died? How do you think the woman died? Was she murdered? Did she commit suicide? Did she die of a broken heart? Give reasons for your answer.
4. What do the final two lines tell you? Comment on how the poet uses wordplay in the final line to emphasise what the poem says about the depth of the man and woman's relationship.

Speaking and listening

❧ In groups, experiment with different ways of reading the poem aloud using one, two or three voices. Discuss the pace of the poem and how the writer uses repetition and wordplay in order to convey the poem's message. Rehearse it, then perform your reading to the rest of the class. Talk about whose performance is the most effective and why.

Writing

❧ Use rhyming couplets to write a poem which is like an epitaph, commemorating the end of a relationship. You could write about the end of either a long and happy marriage, a brief affair or a stormy relationship that ended in separation or divorce. You could use either one or two four-line verses, or pattern your poem as Sir Philip Sidney does.

The evening darkens over

About the poet

Robert Bridges (1844–1930) was educated at Eton and Oxford University, where he rowed for his college. He worked as a surgeon before becoming a full-time writer. He enjoyed experimenting with poetic forms and was a friend of Gerard Manley Hopkins (see page 138), whose poems he edited and published. He also published many essays on literature and language, but they are difficult to read because he had them printed in a phonetic script which he invented. From 1913 to 1930 he was Poet Laureate.

About the poem

In this poem Bridges uses a series of images to describe the loneliness felt by a lover at the end of a relationship. The poem is written in three stanzas of five lines each, the lines varying in length from six to eight syllables. The rhyme schemes of each stanza also vary, but only three rhymes are used in the poem. Before reading the poem, remind yourself what a metaphor is (see page 7).

The evening darkens over

The evening darkens over
After a day so bright
The windcapt waves discover
That wild will be the night.
There's sound of distant thunder. 5

The latest sea-birds hover
Along the cliff's sheer height;
As in the memory wander
Last flutterings of delight,
White wings lost on the white. 10

There's not a ship in sight;
And as the sun goes under
Thick clouds conspire to cover
The moon that should rise yonder.
Thou art alone, fond lover. 15

ROBERT BRIDGES
(1844–1930)

6 *latest* – last
14 *yonder* – over there
15 *fond* – foolish

Activities

Discussion and notemaking

In groups discuss these questions, make notes, then share your ideas in a class discussion.

1. Study the first stanza. What sights and sounds does Bridges describe in this stanza? Which details of the scene are used to suggest that something is coming to an end? What does line 5 suggest about the future and the feelings that may be experienced by the person in the poem?
2. Talk about the second stanza. What further details of the scene are described in lines 6 and 7? Discuss the metaphor that Bridges develops in lines 8–10. What does this suggest about the person's thoughts and feelings?
3. Talk about the third stanza. What details of the scene are described in lines 11–14? How do these details suggest that the relationship is over? Discuss the final sentence of the poem (line 15). What does the phrase 'fond lover' suggest about how the person may be thinking and feeling?
4. How would you describe the mood of the poem? Choose the word(s) from the list below which you think best describes it.
   - sad
   - dejected
   - resigned
   - hopeful
   - wistful
   - pensive
   - melancholic
   - cynical
   - sombre

Speaking and listening

❧ In pairs, rehearse and then tape-record a reading of this poem. Before you begin, discuss what impression you want your reading to have on the listener. What mood will your reading create? If you wish, you could choose a piece of music and/or sound effects either to introduce or act as a background to your reading.

Writing and illustrating

❧ Imagine you are making a film in which this poem is going to be read. Produce a storyboard describing the pictures that you would show while each line is being read. Give details of any music or sound effects that you would include in your soundtrack.

General Questions

Before you begin to answer a question, read each of the poems you think you might use. Look at the notes you made when you studied the poem previously, and read the poem again. Then check that you

- understand what the poem means;
- can say something about your response to a) its tone, b) its language, c) its imagery, and d) its **verse form**;
- have made up your mind about how the poem affects you;
- are ready to support or argue with the poem's **theme**.

If necessary, use the Glossary to check the meaning of any technical terms that you want to use when writing about the poems.

1. The poems in this section present a range of attitudes and ideas about love and relationships. Choose any *two* which express views that you either agree or disagree with. Write a detailed summary of what each poem has to say, quoting any lines that are particularly effective in expressing the poet's viewpoint and saying why you find them effective, then explain why you agree or disagree with the poets' viewpoints.

2. Compare any *three* poems from the section which show how different love poems can be. In making your selection think about romantic and idealised views of love, the range of emotions from extreme happiness to utter despair that lovers can feel, and how love makes people behave. Consider also the wide variety of verse forms that poets use when writing love poems and think about the poets' imagery, techniques and style.

3. It is often claimed that love poems are soppy and sentimental. Referring to the poems that you have studied in this section, find evidence for agreeing or disagreeing with this view. Comment on the language, style and form of the poems you refer to, as well as on their content and viewpoints.

4. Compare *two* poems which describe the poet's memories of first love. Which seems to you to be the more powerful and what is it about the poem which makes it have a greater impact?

5. Do you think that the poems in this section show that men and women have different attitudes to love? Quote from *at least four* poems in your answer.

6. Are any of the feelings towards love shown in these poems very different from feelings which are experienced today? Explain which poems you found the most contemporary in terms of the ideas that they expressed and their language and style, and those which you found the least contemporary.

Conflict

The Flowers of the Forest

About the poet

Jane Elliot (1727–1805) was the daughter of a Scottish baronet and lived the first part of her life at Minto in Teviotdale in the south of Scotland. Later, she moved to Edinburgh, where she lived with her mother and sisters, achieving some notoriety in later life for being the last woman in Edinburgh to make regular use of her own sedan-chair. 'The Flowers of the Forest' is the only poem she is known to have written.

About the poem

'The Flowers of the Forest' is said to have been written one evening in 1756 when Jane and her brother Gilbert were driving home in the family coach. They started to talk about the Battle of Flodden, at which the English defeated the Scots in 1513. Gilbert is said to have bet 'a pair of gloves or a set of ribbons' that his sister could not write a successful ballad about it. According to the story, there was silence for the rest of the journey and by the time it ended Jane had completed a rough draft. It was first published anonymously and was immediately successful.

The poem is written in a Scottish dialect in the form of a traditional ballad, using four-line verses and a strong beat or rhythm to heighten the emotional impact of the story. Each of the verses uses the same rhyme scheme – abab – and there are internal rhymes in lines 1 and 3. The Forest is a district of Selkirk and Peebles, which is in the Scottish Borders. The Flowers are its young men.

The Flowers of the Forest

I've heard them lilting at our ewe-milking,
Lasses a-lilting before the dawn of day;
But now they are moaning on ilka green loaning:–
The Flowers of the Forest are a' wede away.

At bughts in the morning nae blythe lads are scorning; 5
The lasses are lanely, and dowie, and wae;
Nae daffing, nae gabbing, but sighing and sabbing,
Ilk ane lifts her leglin, and hies her away.

In hairst, at the shearing, nae youths now are jeering:
The bandsters are lyart, and runkled, and gray. 10
At fair or at preaching, nae wooing, nae fleeching –
The Flowers of the Forest are a' wede away.

At e'en, in the gloaming, nae swankies are roaming
'Bout stacks wi' the lasses at bogle to play;
But ilk ane sits drearie, lamenting her dearie – 15
The Flowers of the Forest are a' wede away.

Dool and wae for the order sent our lads to the Border
The English, for ance, be guile wan the day;
The Flowers of the Forest, that fought aye the foremost,
The prime of our land, lie cauld in the clay. 20

We'll hear nae mair lilting at our ewe-milking;
Women and bairns are heartless and wae;
Sighing and moaning on ilka green loaning:
The Flowers of the Forest are a' wede away.

JANE ELLIOT
(1727–1805)

1 *lilting* – singing happily
3 *ilka* – every
3 *loaning* – field
4 *a' wede* – all gone
5 *bughts* – sheep-folds
5 *nae* – no
5 *scorning* – good-natured teasing
6 *lanely, dowie, wae* – lonely, sad, woeful
7 *daffing, gabbing, sabbing* – flirting, chatting, sobbing
8 *ilk ane* – each one
8 *leglin* – milk pail
8 *hies* – goes
9 *hairst* – harvest
10 *bandsters* – binders of sheaves of corn
10 *lyart, runkled* – pale, wrinkled
11 *fleeching* – persuading
13 *e'en, gloaming* – evening, twilight
13 *swankies* – young men
14 *'Bout stacks* – round the haystacks
14 *bogle* – hide and seek
17 *Dool and wae* – grief and sadness
18 *ance, be* – once, by
18 *wan* – won
20 *cauld* – cold
21 *mair* – more
22 *bairns* – children

Activities

Discussion and notemaking

First study the poem with a partner, using the notes underneath it to help you with any dialect words you do not understand. Then, discuss these questions, make notes, and share your ideas in a class discussion.

1. What activity does the speaker in the poem focus on in verses 1 and 2? How is it different now from before the young men left? List the words in these lines that describe the young women's grief.
2. In verse 3, she focuses on the harvest, the fair and church-going. How are they different now?
3. In verse 4, what does she say is different about the evenings?
4. What do you learn in verse 5 about why the young men went away to fight, why they lost and how they fought?
5. Compare the last and first verses. How does the last verse echo the first? What further details does it include in order to stress the young women's grief?
6. Which of the verses do you think expresses the young women's grief most effectively? Give reasons for your answer.

Speaking and listening

❧ In groups, experiment with different ways of reading the poem aloud using various combinations of voices, then make a tape-recording of your reading. You could either select an appropriate piece of music to include at the beginning and end of your performance, or use a synthesiser to compose a suitable piece of music.

Writing

❧ Explain how in 'The Flowers of the Forest' Jane Elliot effectively describes the grief and suffering of the women whose lovers or husbands died in the Battle of Flodden. Comment on the language and style of the poem and the use she makes of rhythm, rhyme and repetition to emphasise their feelings of loss.

The Destruction of Sennacherib

About the poet

For details about George Gordon, Lord Byron see page 000.

About the poem

This poem is based on the story of the siege of Jerusalem by Sennacherib, the king of Assyria, which is told in the Bible in the second book of Kings. Jerusalem was spared from destruction by Sennacherib's men after an epidemic of illness amongst his forces:

> And it came to pass that night that the angel of the Lord went out and smote in the camp of the Assyrians an hundred fourscore and five thousand and when they arose early in the morning, behold, they were all dead corpses. (2 Kings, chapter xix, verse 35.)

The poem is written in four-line stanzas each consisting of two rhyming couplets. Each line has twelve syllables and the metre is **anapaestic**. An **anapaest** is a three-syllable metrical foot in which two unstressed syllables are followed by a stressed syllable. The use of this metre helps to give the poem a galloping pace.

The Destruction of Sennacherib

The Assyrian came down like the wolf on the fold,
And his cohorts were gleaming in purple and gold;
And the sheen of their spears was like stars on the sea,
When the blue wave rolls nightly on deep Galilee.

Like the leaves of the forest when Summer is green, 5
That host with their banners at sunset were seen:
Like the leaves of the forest when Autumn hath blown,
That host on the morrow lay wither'd and strown.

For the Angel of Death spread his wings on the blast,
And breathed in the face of the foe as he pass'd; 10
And the eyes of the sleepers wax'd deadly and chill,
And their hearts but once heaved, and for ever grew still!

And there lay the steed with his nostril all wide,
But through it there roll'd not the breath of his pride;
And the foam of his gasping lay white on the turf, 15
And cold as the spray of the rock-beating surf.

And there lay the rider distorted and pale,
With the dew on his brow, and the rust on his mail:
And the tents were all silent, the banners alone,
The lances unlifted, the trumpet unblown. 20

And the widows of Ashur are loud in their wail,
And the idols are broke in the temple of Baal;
And the might of the Gentile, unsmote by the sword,
Hath melted like snow in the glance of the Lord!

George Gordon, Lord Byron
(1788–1824)

2 *cohorts* – bands of soldiers
6 *host* – army
8 *strown* – scattered
9 *blast* – wind
11 *wax'd deadly* – grew death-like
13 *steed* – horse
18 *mail* – armour
21 *Ashur* – Assyrian capital, named after sun-god
22 *Baal* – male heathen god
23 *Gentile* – i.e. not Jewish
23 *unsmote* – not struck

Activities

Discussion and notemaking

Discuss these questions in groups. Each make notes of your ideas, then share them in a class discussion.

1. What impression do you get of the Assyrian army from verse 1? What do the similes in lines 1 and 3–4 suggest about them?
2. What pictures of the Assyrian army are created by the two similes that Byron uses in verse 2? Discuss how the contrast helps to convey the suddenness of what has happened to them overnight.
3. What does verse 3 say about how the Assyrians died?
4. List the details of the Assyrian camp that are described in verses 4 and 5. Pick out the words and phrases which suggest that the scene is silent and lifeless.
5. What does verse 6 tell you about how the Assyrians react to the destruction of their army? Discuss the final two lines of the poem and the simile that Byron uses to suggest who has been responsible for the destruction of the Assyrian army.

Speaking and listening

❧ In groups, discuss how the verse form is suitable to the story which Byron is telling, and how it helps to keep the poem moving at a fast pace. Experiment with different ways of reading the poem aloud, using various combinations of voices. Decide which combination works best, then rehearse a performance of the poem and either tape-record it or present it to the rest of the class. Compare your different performances and decide whose performance was the most effective.

❧ In groups of three, prepare a news broadcast for either Jerusalem radio or television in which a news presenter gives details of the destruction of the Assyrian army, an on-the-spot reporter in the Assyrian camp describes the scene, and a Jewish leader gives his reaction to the news.

The Eve of Waterloo

About the poet

For details of George Gordon, Lord Byron see page 30.

About the poem

This is an extract from a longer poem, 'Childe Harold's Pilgrimage', in which a pilgrim, disgusted with a life of pleasure and revelry, journeys through Europe and reflects upon the historical events that have occurred in the places he visits. In this section of the poem he is visiting Brussels and thinking about the ball that was given there by the Duchess of Richmond on 15 June 1815. This was the evening when the British troops began the advance that led to the Battle of Waterloo on 18 June 1815, at which the French emperor Napoleon was defeated. The ball was attended by British and Prussian officers, including the British commander the Duke of Wellington, who appeared there after he had already given orders for the army to march on the village of Quatre Bras, where a battle took place the following day. Wellington revealed nothing by his manner, but news of the troops' movement spread quickly and the officers gradually left.

The poem is written in verses known as **Spenserian stanzas**, because they were invented by the Elizabethan poet Edmund Spenser (*c.*1552–99) for his long poem 'The Faerie Queene'.

Each stanza consists of nine lines – eight 10-syllable lines (pentameters) and a final 12-syllable line (**hexameter**). The rhyme scheme of each stanza is ababbcbcc.

The Eve of Waterloo

There was a sound of revelry by night,
And Belgium's capital had gathered then
Her Beauty and her Chivalry, and bright
The lamps shone o'er fair women and brave men,
A thousand hearts beat happily; and when 5
Music arose with its voluptuous swell,
Soft eyes looked love to eyes which spake again,
And all went merry as a marriage bell;
But hush! hark! a deep sound strikes like a rising knell!

Did ye not hear it? – No; 'twas but the wind, 10
Or the car rattling o'er the stony street;
On with the dance! let joy be unconfined;
No sleep till morn, when Youth and Pleasure meet
To chase the glowing hours with flying feet –
But hark! – that heavy sound breaks in once more, 15
As if the clouds its echo would repeat;
And nearer, clearer, deadlier than before!
Arm! Arm! it is – it is – the cannon's opening roar!

Within a window'd niche of that high hall
Sate Brunswick's fated chieftain; he did hear 20
That sound the first amidst the festival,
And caught its tone with Death's prophetic ear;
And when they smiled because he deemed it near,
His heart more truly knew that peal too well
Which stretched his father on a bloody bier, 25
And roused the vengeance blood alone could quell;
He rushed into the field, and, foremost fighting, fell.

Ah! then and there was hurrying to and fro,
And gathering tears, and tremblings of distress,
And cheeks all pale, which but an hour ago 30
Blushed at the praise of their own loveliness;
And there were sudden partings, such as press
The life from out young hearts, and choking sighs
Which ne'er might be repeated; who could guess
If ever more should meet those mutual eyes, 35
Since upon night so sweet such awful morn could rise!

And there was mounting in hot haste: the steed,
The mustering squadron, and the clattering car,
Went pouring forward with impetuous speed,
And swiftly forming in the ranks of war; 40
And the deep thunder peal on peal afar;
And near, the beat of the alarming drum
Roused up the soldier ere the morning star;
While thronged the citizens with terror dumb,
Or whispering, with white lips – 'The foe! they come! they come!' 45

And wild and high the 'Cameron's gathering' rose!
The war-note of Lochiel, which Albyn's hills
Have heard, and heard, too, have her Saxon foes:–
How in the noon of night that pibroch thrills,
Savage and shrill! But with the breath which fills 50
Their mountain-pipe, so fill the mountaineers
With the fierce native daring which instils
The stirring memory of a thousand years,
And Evan's, Donald's fame rings in each clansman's ears!

And Ardennes waves above them her green leaves, 55
Dewy with nature's tear-drops as they pass,
Grieving, if aught inanimate e'er grieves,
Over the unreturning brave, – alas!
Ere evening to be trodden like the grass
Which now beneath them, but above shall grow 60
In its next verdure, when this fiery mass
Of living valour, rolling on the foe,
And burning with high hope shall moulder cold and low.

Last noon beheld them full of lusty life,
Last eve in Beauty's circle proudly gay, 65
The midnight brought the signal-sound of strife,
The morn the marshalling in arms, – the day
Battle's magnificently stern array!
The thunder-clouds close o'er it, which when rent
The earth is covered thick with other clay, 70
Which her own clay shall cover, heaped and pent,
Rider and horse, – friend, foe, – in one red burial blent!

GEORGE GORDON, LORD BYRON
(1788–1824)

3 *Chivalry* – aristocracy
6 *voluptuous* – senses-pleasing
9 *knell* – funeral bell
11 *car* – carriage
20 *sate* – sat
20 *fated* – ill-fated
25 *bier* – wooden frame on which a corpse is placed
38 *mustering squadron* – assembling cavalry
44 *ere* – before
46 *Cameron's gathering* – martial tune on the bagpipes
47 *Albyn's* – Scotland's
49 *pibroch* – martial tune for bagpipes
55 *Ardennes* – forest on frontier of Belgium and France
57 *aught* – anything
61 *verdure* – green growth
63 *moulder* – decay
64 *lusty* – healthy and strong
68 *array* – line-up
69 *rent* – broken
70 *other clay* – bodies
71 *pent* – enclosed
72 *blent* – mixed

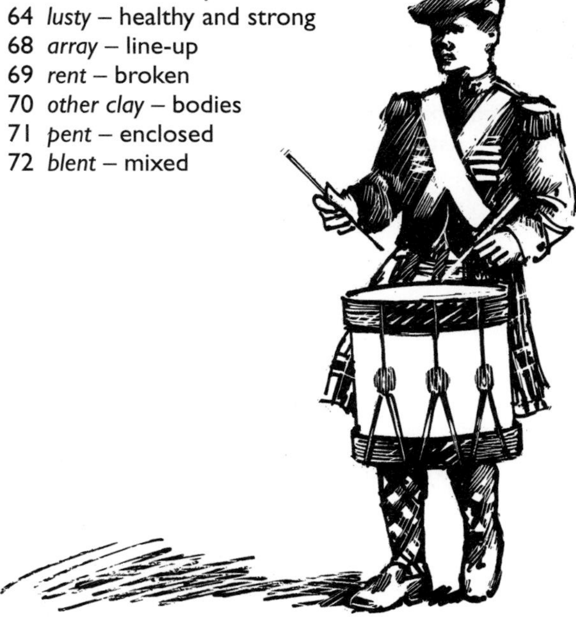

Activities

Discussion and notemaking

In groups discuss these questions. Make notes of your answers on each stanza, then share your ideas in a class discussion.

1. List the words and phrases in stanza 1 which Byron uses to create a picture of gaiety and happiness. Discuss the simile he uses in line 9 and how line 9 abruptly changes the mood that has been created in the rest of the stanza.

2. In the second stanza, how does Byron show that at first the people at the ball prefer not to recognise the sound for what it is? Discuss how the sound is described in lines 15–18 so that by the end of the stanza they have no choice but to admit what is happening.
3. What effect does Byron suggest the sound has on the Duke of Brunswick (stanza 3)? Why does he react to it more quickly than others at the ball? List the words and phrases in lines 19–26 that Byron uses to suggest Brunswick's forthcoming death.
4. What scenes are described in stanza 4? How does Byron show that the mood at the ball has changed completely?
5. What sights and sounds are described in stanza 5? How does Byron create a picture of an army hurriedly getting ready for battle and of a crowd of civilians watching anxiously?
6. What sound is described in stanza 6? What effect does Byron say it has on the clansmen who hear it?
7. Discuss how the images that Byron uses in stanza 7 express sadness at the death towards which many of the soldiers are marching.
8. Discuss how in the first five lines of stanza 8 (lines 64–68) Byron summarises the events from noon on the eve of the battle to dawn on the day of the battle. What images does he use in lines 69–72 to describe the consequences of the battle?

Speaking and listening

❧ In groups, make a tape-recording of this poem. First, discuss what impression you want each stanza to create on the listener, and then experiment with different ways of reading the stanzas in order to achieve those effects. Next, list all the sound effects that you could include to accompany your reading of the poem, and rehearse the reading with the sound effects before making your recording. Listen to the tape-recordings and decide whose is the most effective and why.

❧ On your own, script and deliver an on-the-spot report from a journalist in Brussels who has interviewed someone who was at the ball, spoken to some of the officers as they left, and is watching the troops as they set off for Quatre Bras.

Writing

❧ Imagine that you have been commissioned to edit a book of 'Poems with Pictures' and asked to instruct either an artist or a photographer to produce a series of up to 12 pictures to illustrate 'The Eve of Waterloo'. Write a detailed brief for the artist or photographer describing the pictures or photographs you want them to produce.

❧ Write notes to show your understanding of Byron's effective use of detail in 'The Eve of Waterloo', and of the changing emotions evoked by the poem.

Drummer Hodge

About the poet

Thomas Hardy (1840–1928) is famous for novels such as *Under the Greenwood Tree* and *Tess of the D'Urbervilles*, set in the countryside in and around Dorset, which he called Wessex. After his novel *Jude the Obscure* received strongly unfavourable reviews, he gave up writing fiction and turned to poetry, which had been a constant interest. From 1898 onwards he published seven volumes of lyric poetry, containing poems written in a wide variety of forms and including outstanding love poetry written in old age about his wife, by then dead.

About the poem

The Boer War took place from 1899 to 1902 in South Africa. The British, who controlled the colonies of Natal and Cape Colony, fought against the descendants of the early Dutch settlers, the Boers, who came from the independent republics of the Transvaal and the Orange Free State.

In this poem Hardy writes about the death of a drummer boy during the Boer War. Until the twentieth century, it was traditional for armies to march into battle to the beat of a drum, often played by a young recruit. The drummer boy was unarmed and, therefore, more likely to get killed in the hand-to-hand fighting that was usual in pre-twentieth-century battles.

'Drummer Hodge' was first published in December 1899 under the title 'The Dead Drummer'.

Drummer Hodge

They throw in Drummer Hodge, to rest
   Uncoffined – just as found:
His landmark is a kopje-crest
   That breaks the veldt around;
And foreign constellations west   5
   Each night above his mound.

Young Hodge the Drummer never knew –
   Fresh from his Wessex home –
The meaning of the broad Karoo,
   The Bush, the dusty loam   10
And why uprose to nightly view
   Strange stars amid the gloam.

Yet portion of that unknown plain
Will Hodge for ever be;
His homely Northern breast and brain 15
Grow to some Southern tree,
And strange-eyed constellations reign
His stars eternally.

THOMAS HARDY
(1840–1928)

3 *kopje* – South African hill
4 *veldt* – grassland (S. African word)
9 *Karoo* – elevated plateau (S. African word)
12 *gloam* – darkness

Activities

Discussion and notemaking

Discuss these questions in pairs, each making notes of your ideas, and then share them in either a group or class discussion.

1. What does the poet tell you in lines 1 and 2 about Hodge's burial and how he was buried?
2. What do you learn from lines 3–6 about where Hodge was buried?
3. What do lines 7–12 tell you about where Hodge came from and what he knew about the place he was sent to fight in? What impression does this verse give you of Hodge?
4. Notice how in lines 13–18 the poet contrasts the place where Hodge lived with the place where he is buried. What does this suggest about Hardy's view of Hodge's fate?

Writing

❧ Draft a paragraph saying what view of the young drummer's death and of his burial in a foreign land is presented by Thomas Hardy in this poem. When you have finished, form groups, read each other's paragraphs, and discuss your ideas. Then, each revise what you have written, and make a wall display of your responses to the poem.

Epitaph on an Army of Mercenaries

About the poet

Although he was a dedicated classics student, A. E. Housman (1859–1936) failed his degree at Oxford University because he was not interested in philosophy. Nevertheless, he went on to become a distinguished scholar and Professor of Latin at University College, London. In a famous lecture on poetry in 1933, he shocked his audience by claiming that the excitement felt when either writing or reading poetry is a physical experience which has almost no connection with the poem's 'meaning'.

About the poem

This poem was first published in *The Times*. It appeared on 31 October 1917, the third anniversary of the first Battle of Ypres (19 October – 22 November 1914). The 'mercenaries' were the soldiers of the professional English army, known as the British Expeditionary Force, who were sent to France in 1914. They were nicknamed the Old Contemptibles, because the German Emperor Wilhelm II is supposed to have referred to the British Expeditionary Force as 'a contemptible little army'. At Ypres they were outnumbered by the German army and suffered heavy casualties, but managed to restrict the Germans to only gradual advances.

An epitaph is a commemorative inscription which is written on a tomb or monument, or a poem remembering the dead.

Epitaph on an Army of Mercenaries

These, in the day when heaven was falling,
   The hour when earth's foundations fled,
Followed their mercenary calling
   And took their wages and are dead.

Their shoulders held the sky suspended;   5
   They stood, and earth's foundations stay;
What God abandoned, these defended,
   And saved the sum of things for pay.

A. E. HOUSMAN
(1859–1936)

Mercenaries – soldiers fighting for the money

Activities

Discussion and notemaking

Study the poem on your own and think about these three questions. Note down your ideas, then share them in a group discussion.

1. What impression does the poem give of the mercenaries? Which word(s) from the list below best describe your impression of them? Can you suggest any others?
   - avaricious
   - courageous
   - foolhardy
   - unselfish
   - dauntless
   - steadfast
   - unprincipled
   - resolute
   - indifferent
   - stout-hearted
2. What does the poem tell you about the mercenaries' attitude towards fighting?
3. Study lines 7–8. What is the poet's attitude towards the army of mercenaries? Does he
   - respect them?
   - despise them?
   - pity them?
   - admire them?

Quote evidence from the poem to support your views.

Speaking and listening

❧ Role play a scene in which two people with different viewpoints, e.g. an ex-professional soldier and a conscientious objector, discuss their different reactions to Housman's poem.

Writing

❧ A Scottish poet, Christopher Murray Grieve (1892–1978), who wrote under the pseudonym Hugh McDiarmid, was prompted to write another epitaph expressing a different view of mercenaries. 'Another Epitaph on an Army of Mercenaries' appeared in a book of his poems that was published in 1935. Study McDiarmid's poem (below) and compare it with Housman's poem. Then write about the two poems explaining their different viewpoints and commenting on the language and style of the poems.

Another Epitaph on an Army of Mercenaries

It is a God-damned lie to say that these
Saved, or knew, anything worth any man's pride.
They were professional murderers and they took
Their blood-money, and impious risks, and died.
In spite of all their kind, some elements of worth
Persist with difficulty here and there on earth.

❧ Draft a poem of your own, using the form of an epitaph, on the death of either a conscript or a volunteer. Then, draft a second epitaph expressing a contrasting view of the conscript's or the volunteer's death.

The Soldier

About the poet

Rupert Brooke (1887–1915) was educated at Rugby and Cambridge University. His first book of poems was published in 1911, and his youth and charm had already won him a wide circle of friends prior to the outbreak of the First World War in 1914. Like many young men of his generation, Brooke was fired by patriotism and enthusiastically volunteered. He was commissioned into the Royal Navy Division, but died of blood-poisoning on the way to fight in Gallipoli and was buried on the Greek island of Skyros. His obituary in *The Times* was written by Winston Churchill.

About the poem

This is an autobiographical poem in which Brooke uses the sonnet form to express a personal viewpoint. It was written in 1914 and published in 1915.

The poem is a Petrarchan sonnet (see page 12). The rhyme scheme is ababcdcd efgefg.

The Soldier

If I should die, think only this of me:
  That there's some corner of a foreign field
That is for ever England. There shall be
  In that rich earth a richer dust concealed;
A dust whom England bore, shaped, made aware, 5
  Gave, once, her flowers to love, her ways to roam,
A body of England's, breathing English air,
  Washed by the rivers, blest by the suns of home.

And think, this heart, all evil shed away,
  A pulse in the eternal mind, no less 10
    Gives somewhere back the thoughts by England given;
Her sights and sounds; dreams happy as her day;
  And laughter, learnt of friends; and gentleness,
    In hearts at peace, under an English heaven.

Rupert Brooke
(1887–1915)

Activities

Discussion and notemaking

Discuss these questions in groups, each making notes of your ideas and then share them in a class discussion.

1. What audience do you think Brooke is speaking to in this sonnet?
2. What does he want people to think about him if he dies and is buried in a foreign land?
3. What does he mean by the phrase 'a richer dust'? (line 4) How do lines 5–8 explain why he thinks it is richer?
4. Discuss how the thought develops and changes in the last six lines of the sonnet. What does he ask people, instead of grieving for him, to think about how his Englishness will be preserved?
5. How would you sum up the mood of this sonnet? Choose any words from the following list which you think describe it. Can you suggest any others? Give reasons for your views.
   - hopeful
   - morbid
   - sentimental
   - patriotic
   - melancholic
   - nostalgic
   - jingoistic
   - unselfish
   - courageous
   - foolhardy

Speaking and listening

❧ Use your notes on 'An Epitaph for an Army of Mercenaries', and your notes on Brooke's poem, to help you draft part of a presentation for an assembly on Remembrance Day in memory of those who sacrificed their lives for their country in the First World War. Then, form groups and compare your speeches.

❧ Work with a partner and each rehearse a reading of the poem. Discuss what impression you want your reading to create and whether you want it to be sympathetic or unsympathetic to Brooke's views. Decide how you are going to speak the lines in order to show the change of mood between the octave (lines 1–8) and the sestet (lines 9–16). Then form groups, perform your readings, and discuss how effective they are.

Writing

❧ Compare the thoughts and feelings that Hardy expresses about the death of a soldier in his poem 'Drummer Hodge' with the thoughts and feelings that Brooke expresses in this poem. Which do you think is the more effective? Explain why.

❧ Explain how the structure of the Petrarchan sonnet with its break between the octave and the sestet suits the development of the thoughts and feelings in Rupert Brooke's 'The Soldier'.

Ambulance Train

About the poet

Wilfrid Wilson Gibson (1878–1962) was born in Hexham, Northumberland and educated privately. He served as a private in the First World War, having been rejected four times because of poor sight. He was a friend of Rupert Brooke (see page 61), who called him 'Wibson', and with him was one of the poets published in the anthology *Georgian Poetry 1911–1912*, which sold 15,000 copies. He was a prolific poet throughout his long life. His early poems often deal with the daily lives and hardships of ordinary people. Later poems show an understanding of the suffering war causes. He wrote the well-known literary ballad, 'Flannan Isle'.

About the poem

In this poem W. W. Gibson describes the thoughts of a person accompanying injured men on an ambulance train. He uses short regular six-syllable lines and the repetition of lines and rhymes (note that he uses only two rhymes) to recreate the rhythm and motion of the train.

Before you read the poem, remind yourself what alliteration is (see page 18).

Ambulance Train

Red rowans in the rain
Above the rain-wet rock –
All night the lumbering train
With jolt and jar and shock,
And moan of men in pain, 5
Beats rumbling in my brain –
Red rowans in the rain
Above the rain-wet rock –
Again and yet again,
Red rowans in the rain. 10

WILFRID WILSON GIBSON
(1878–1962)

1 *rowans* – trees, also known as mountains ashes, with scarlet berries

Activities

Discussion and notemaking

Discuss these question in pairs. Each make notes of your ideas, then share them in a class discussion.

1. Why does the man in the poem keep remembering the rowans? What is suggested by the image of the 'red rowans in the rain'?
2. Discuss how in lines 3 and 4 the poet creates the impression that the train is moving slowly and jerkily.
3. Which lines tell you that the man in the poem cannot get the wounded soldiers, the sound of the train or the image of the rowans out of his mind?
4. Discuss how Gibson uses alliteration and repetition to suggest the sound and movement of the train.
5. Imagine that you have been asked to find a number of photographs to illustrate this poem. Explain in detail what photographs you would use.
6. What thoughts and feelings about the suffering of the injured soldiers are you left with as a result of reading and studying this poem?

Speaking and listening

❧ In groups, each take it in turn to prepare and then to perform a reading of the poem. Decide whose reading most effectively captures both the rhythm of the train and the suffering of its passengers.

Writing

❧ Draft a short poem of your own in which, like W. W. Gibson, you use a single image to express the pain and suffering of soldiers who have been wounded.

Spreading Manure

About the poet

Rose Macaulay (1881–1958) is more famous for her novels and her travel writing than for her poetry. She wrote 23 novels, including the prize-winning *The Towers of Trebizond*, published in 1956. She also wrote several books of literary criticism and, as a journalist, contributed articles to newspapers and magazines such as the *Observer* and the *Spectator*. Throughout the First World War she worked as a civil servant.

From 1918 until his death in 1942 she had a secret affair with the Irish writer, Gerald O'Donovan, who was married and an ex-priest.

About the poem

In this poem Rose Macaulay describes the thoughts of a land-girl – one of the many women who spent the war working as farm labourers, taking the place of men who had joined the army.

The poem is written in quatrains with the rhyme scheme abab. The first and third lines are longer than the second and fourth lines, but there is no regular metre.

Spreading Manure

There are forty steaming heaps in the one tree field,
   Lying in four rows of ten,
They must be all spread out ere the earth will yield
   As it should (and it won't, even then).

Drive the great fork in, fling it out wide; 5
   Jerk it with a shoulder throw,
The stuff must lie even, two feet on each side.
   Not in patches, but level … so!

When the heap is thrown you must go all round
   And flatten it out with the spade, 10
It must lie quite close and trim till the ground
   Is like bread spread with marmalade.

The north-east wind stabs and cuts our breaths,
The soaked clay numbs our feet,
We are palsied like people gripped by death 15
In the beating of the frozen sleet.

I think no soldier is so cold as we,
Sitting in the frozen mud.
I wish I was out there, for it might be
A shell would burst to heat my blood. 20

I wish I was out there, for I should creep
In my dug-out and hide my head,
I should feel no cold when they lay me deep
To sleep in a six-foot bed.

I wish I was out there, and off the open land: 25
A deep trench I could just endure.
But things being other, I needs must stand
Frozen, and spread wet manure.

ROSE MACAULAY
(1881–1958)

3 *ere* – before
15 *palsied* – paralysed

Activities

Discussion and notemaking

First, read the poem on your own. What pictures do you get from the poem of a land-girl's life? Draw two columns, then list your impressions in one column and the lines/verse which give you those ideas in the other. Next, discuss what you have written with a partner before working together to make notes in answer to these questions.

1. What do you learn from the first three verses about the work the land-girl has to do?
2. What does verse 4 tell you about the conditions in which she is working? What does the simile in lines 15–16 tell you about the effect the conditions have on the land-girls?
3. What do the final three verses tell you about how the land-girl feels about working in such conditions?
4. What does line 20 show of the land-girl's understanding of actual trench-warfare?

5. What do you think Rose Macaulay's attitude towards the land-girl is? Do you think she sympathises with her for working in such unpleasant conditions? Or do you think she is satirising her for complaining, while others are away at the Front risking their lives? Give reasons for your views.

Speaking and listening

❧ In groups, role play a conversation between two land-girls and two soldiers' wives in which an argument develops because the land-girls start complaining about the conditions in which they have to work and comparing them to life in the trenches.

Writing

❧ Draft a poem about a young soldier digging a trench in damp, freezing conditions and wishing he was back home working on the farm. You could either choose your own verse form or use the same verse form as Rose Macaulay.

Disabled

About the poet

Wilfred Owen (1893–1918) served as an officer in the trenches during the First World War. He was invalided home in 1917 and sent to Craiglockhart War Hospital near Edinburgh, where he met Siegfried Sassoon (see page 72). Sassoon encouraged Owen to write, sometimes reading and commenting on drafts of Owen's poems. In 1918, Owen returned to the Front and in October was awarded the Military Cross. He was killed a week before the Armistice, which ended the First World War, was signed. Owen's poems were published posthumously in 1920, with an introduction written by Sassoon.

About the poem

In this poem an omniscient narrator (i.e. someone who knows everything which his characters do, feel or think) reveals the thoughts and feelings of a severely disabled soldier as he sits in a wheelchair waiting for the nurses to come and put him into bed. The poem was written shortly after a meeting between Owen and Robert Graves, who subsequently became famous for his autobiographical account of his wartime experiences, *Goodbye To All That*.

Disabled

He sat in a wheeled chair, waiting for dark,
And shivered in his ghastly suit of grey,
Legless, sewn short at elbow. Through the park
Voices of boys rang saddening like a hymn,
Voices of play and pleasure after day, 5
Till gathering sleep had mothered them from him.

About this time Town used to swing so gay
When glow-lamps budded in the light blue trees,
And girls glanced lovelier as the air grew dim, –
In the old times, before he threw away his knees. 10
Now he will never feel again how slim
Girls' waists are, or how warm their subtle hands;
All of them touch him like some queer disease.

There was an artist silly for his face,
For it was younger than his youth, last year. 15
Now, he is old; his back will never brace;
He's lost his colour very far from here,
Poured it down shell-holes till the veins ran dry,
And half his lifetime lapsed in the hot race
And leap of purple spurted from his thigh. 20

One time he liked a blood-smear down his leg,
After the matches, carried shoulder-high.
It was after football, when he'd drunk a peg,
He thought he'd better join. – He wonders why.
Someone had said he'd look a god in kilts, 25
That's why; and maybe, too, to please his Meg;
Aye, that was it, to please the giddy jilts
He asked to join. He didn't have to beg;
Smiling they wrote his lie: aged nineteen years.
Germans he scarcely thought of; all their guilt, 30
And Austria's, did not move him. And no fears
Of Fear came yet. He thought of jewelled hilts
For daggers in plaid socks; of smart salutes;
And care of arms; and leave; and pay arrears;
Esprit de corps; and hints for young recruits. 35
And soon, he was drafted out with drums and cheers.

Some cheered him home, but not as crowds cheer Goal.
Only a solemn man who brought him fruits
Thanked him; and then enquired about his soul.

Now, he will spend a few sick years in institutes, 40
And do what things the rules consider wise,
And take whatever pity they may dole.
Tonight he noticed how the women's eyes
Passed from him to the strong men that were whole.
How cold and late it is! Why don't they come 45
And put him into bed? Why don't they come?

Wilfred Owen
(1893–1918)

12 *subtle* – tender
14 *artist silly for his face* – youth younger than his looks
16 *brace* – be straight
23 *peg* – brandy-and-soda
27 *giddy jilts* – flirtatious young women
35 *esprit de corps* – pride in his regiment
42 *dole* – hand out

Activities

Discussion and notemaking

Read the poem through twice on your own and use four headings under which to note down a) your impression of the young man, b) what he used to be like, c) what he is like now, and d) what the future holds for him. Then note down what impression you get of people's attitudes towards him.

Discuss your notes and ideas with a partner and together study the poem section by section. Each make notes of your answers to these questions, then share your ideas in a class discussion.

Section 1 (lines 1–6)

1. What picture of the young man is given in lines 1–3? Why is he 'waiting for dark'?
2. Suggest what he is thinking and feeling as he hears the voices of boys playing in the park. What does the simile in line 4 suggest?

Section 2 (lines 7–20)

3. What do lines 7–12 tell you about how his life has been changed by the injuries he has received?
4. What do you learn from line 13 about how girls regard him now?
5. What do lines 14–16 tell you about how his injuries have changed him?
6. Discuss lines 17–20. What image do they create of him being wounded? Which words and phrases emphasise what he lost?

Section 3 (lines 21–36)

7. What do lines 21–22 tell you about the young man? What picture do these lines create and how does it contrast with the picture given in lines 17–20?
8. What made the young man decide to join up (lines 23–28)?
9. How was he treated when he volunteered (lines 28–29)? What do you learn about him in line 29?
10. What view of war and of being a soldier did the young man have when he joined up (lines 30–35)?
11. What attitude did people have towards him when he left to go to the Front (line 36)?

Section 4 (lines 37–39)

12. How was he greeted on his return (line 36)?
13. Who is the solemn man (line 38)? How does the young man feel about his visit?

Section 5 (lines 40–46)

14. What do lines 40–42 tell you about what he thinks the future holds now that he is so disabled?
15. What does he notice about the way women look at him (lines 43–44)? Why do you think he wants the nurses to come and put him into bed?

Speaking and listening

❧ Role play a scene in which two people talk about the young disabled man. One of them is a nurse at the hospital where he is being cared for, the other is a person who knew him before the war and has been to visit him. Together discuss the injuries he has received, what he used to be like, and what the future holds for him. When you have finished, discuss how you felt as you role-played the scene.

❧ Then, take it in turns to perform your role plays to the rest of the class. Decide which role play most effectively portrays the young man's situation.

Writing

❧ Explain how in this poem Owen uses the story of a wounded soldier to make a powerful statement about how war can destroy a person's life.

❧ 'In his poem "Disabled", Wilfred Owen is protesting not only about what war does to people, but also about people's attitudes towards war and those whose lives are ruined by it.' Say whether you agree or disagree with this statement, using evidence from the poem to support your view.

Suicide in the Trenches

About the poet

As a young man Siegfried Sassoon (1886–1967) spent more time playing tennis, hunting and writing poetry than studying, and left Cambridge University without getting a degree. During the First World War he served as an officer, showing exceptional bravery and being awarded the Military Cross for capturing a German trench single-handed. He was wounded and invalided home, where the horrors he had witnessed led him to make a public protest against the continuation of the war, including throwing his Military Cross medal into the River Mersey. Instead of being court-martialled he was sent to Craiglockhart War Hospital, and later returned to the Front. After the war, he continued writing poetry, and became famous for *Memoirs of a Fox-Hunting Man* and *Memoirs of an Infantry Officer*, autobiographical accounts of his early life and his wartime experiences.

About the poem

In this poem Sassoon tells the story of a young man driven to commit suicide by life in the trenches. Each verse has four lines and the rhyme scheme aabb.

Suicide in the Trenches

I knew a simple soldier boy
Who grinned at life in empty joy,
Slept soundly through the lonesome dark,
And whistled early with the lark.

In winter trenches, cowed and glum, 5
With crumps and lice and lack of rum,
He put a bullet through his brain.
No one spoke of him again.

. . . .

You smug-faced crowds with kindling eye
Who cheer when soldier lads march by, 10
Sneak home and pray you'll never know
The hell where youth and laughter go.

SIEGFRIED SASSOON
(1886–1967)

6 *crumps* – sounds of bursting shells (**onomatopoeia**)
9 *kindling* – showing emotion

Activities

Discussion and notemaking

On your own, write notes in answer to these questions, then share your ideas in a group discussion.

1. In the first verse, what picture does Sassoon give of the young man? Pick out the words and phrases which create that impression.
2. What do you learn from lines 5 and 6 about why the young soldier committed suicide?
3. What does line 8 tell you about people's reaction to the young man's suicide? Why do they react in this way? Do you think the poet approves of their behaviour? Give reasons for your view.
4. Who is Sassoon addressing in the final verse? What is his attitude towards them? Pick out the words and phrases which tell you what he thinks of them.
5. In your own words, sum up what Sassoon is telling people about life in the trenches in the last two lines.
6. Comment on the language and style of the poem, in particular how Sassoon writes simply and directly. Choose two or three key words or phrases from each verse and discuss the effect they achieve.

Speaking and listening

❧ In pairs, act out a scene in which two people express different views about a young soldier who has committed suicide in the trenches. One of the people, a soldier with experience of the trenches, like Sassoon adopts an understanding attitude, while the other, a civilian, condemns the dead soldier as a coward.

Writing

❧ Write two contrasting letters to the young soldier's mother about his death – one written by his Commanding Officer, the other by an ordinary soldier who was a family friend.

An Irish Airman Foresees His Death

About the poet

W. B. Yeats (1865–1939) was an Irish poet, playwright and senator. As a young man he became interested in Far Eastern religion and in magic, and subsequently wrote a book about occult philosophy. He played an important part in setting up the famous Abbey Theatre in Dublin and in encouraging Irish culture and writing about Irish life. In 1923, he was awarded the Nobel Prize for Literature. About the craft of writing, Yeats wrote in one of his poems:

> A line will take us hours maybe;
> Yet if it does not seem a moment's thought
> Our stitching and unstitching has been nought.

About the poem

This is one of four poems which Yeats wrote in memory of Major Robert Gregory. Ireland was a neutral country during the First World War, and although Gregory was Irish and therefore himself neutral, he nevertheless became a member of the British Royal Flying Corps. He was killed in action on 23 January 1918. The poem takes the form of a dramatic monologue, as if Robert Gregory is speaking his thoughts aloud. Although the poem is not divided into stanzas, it has regular eight-syllable lines and each four-line section has lines which rhyme alternately.

An Irish Airman Foresees His Death

I know that I shall meet my fate
Somewhere among the clouds above;
Those that I fight I do not hate,
Those that I guard I do not love;
My country is Kiltartan Cross, 5
My countrymen Kiltartan's poor,
No likely end could bring them loss
Or leave them happier than before.
Nor law, nor duty bade me fight,
Nor public men, nor cheering crowds, 10
A lonely impulse of delight
Drove to this tumult in the clouds;
I balanced all, brought all to mind,
The years to come seemed waste of breath,
A waste of breath the years behind 15
In balance with this life, this death.

W. B. YEATS
(1865–1939)

3 i.e. the Germans
4 i.e. the British
9 *bade* – ordered
10 *public men* – politicians
12 *tumult* – a conflict of emotions

Activities

Discussion and notemaking

In this poem, Yeats shows Gregory explaining why he chose to fight even though he foresaw that he would be killed.

On your own, study the poem and draw a flow chart to show the development of Gregory's thoughts through the poem. Then, in pairs, compare your flow charts and discuss the questions below. Make notes of your answers, then share your ideas in a class discussion.

1. What do you learn from lines 3 and 4 about Gregory's attitude to those he is fighting against and those he is fighting for?
2. In lines 5–8 what effect does he suggest his death will have on his fellow-countrymen?
3. What do you learn about his motives for volunteering from lines 9–12? What do you think he means by the phrase 'a lonely impulse of delight' (line 11)?
4. What do lines 13–16 tell you about Gregory's thoughts about his past life and what the future holds for him? How do these lines help to explain the choice he made?
5. How would you describe Gregory's feelings about the death that he foresees for himself? Which of these words sums up his feelings?
   - resignation
   - sorrow
   - despair
   - acceptance
   - regret
   - elation

Give reasons for your answer.

Speaking and listening

❧ Rehearse reading the poem aloud on your own, then join up with others into a group and present your reading to the rest of your group. Concentrate on using the pace and rhythm of the poem in your reading to capture the mood of the person speaking. Then choose one of your readings to present to the rest of the class, and discuss which readings you preferred and why.

Reconciliation

About the poet

For details of Siegfried Sassoon see page 72.

About the poem

This poem was written in November 1918, the month in which the Armistice was signed.

Reconciliation

When you are standing at your hero's grave,
Or near some homeless village where he died,
Remember, through your heart's rekindling pride,
The German soldiers who were loyal and brave.

Men fought like brutes; and hideous things were done, 5
And you have nourished hatred, harsh and blind.
But in that Golgotha perhaps you'll find
The mothers of the men who killed your son.

SIEGRIED SASSOON
(1886–1967)

7 *Golgotha* – place of suffering and death (see St Mark, chapter 15, verse 22)

Activities

Discussion and notemaking

Work through these questions on your own, making notes of your answers, then share your ideas in either a group or class discussion.

1. Who are the people Sassoon is addressing in verse 1? Where are they and what are they doing? What does the phrase 'your heart's rekindling pride' suggest about their feelings?
2. Who else does Sassoon ask the people to remember (line 4)?
3. What does he say in line 5 about the war and how people behaved?
4. In line 6 what does he say about the feelings that the war has created in the people he is addressing?
5. Who does he suggest they might meet (lines 7 and 8)? What would those people be doing there?
6. What does the title suggest that the poet hopes will result from their meeting?

Speaking and listening

❧ Role play a conversation between an English mother and a German mother who meet after visiting their sons' graves. Before you begin, discuss the different ways that the mothers might behave and act out the scene several times to show their different reactions. Then, share what you have learned from this activity in a group discussion.

Writing

❧ Show how in poems such as 'Suicide in the Trenches' (see page 72) and 'Reconciliation' Sassoon conveys his ideas about war and its effects simply and directly.

Futility

About the poet

For details of Wilfred Owen see page 68.

About the poem

This poem was written in 1918. In it the speaker reflects on the death of a soldier who has recently been killed.

The poem consists of two 7-line stanzas with the same rhyme scheme ababccc. The first and last lines of each stanza have six syllables, whereas all the other lines have eight. Many of the rhymes that Owen uses are near-rhymes or **half-rhymes** rather than complete rhymes, e.g. 'sun' and 'unsown' and 'once' and 'France' in the first stanza, and 'star' and 'stir' in the second stanza.

Futility

Move him into the sun –
Gently its touch awoke him once,
At home, whispering of fields unsown.
Always it woke him, even in France,
Until this morning and this snow. 5
If anything might rouse him now
The kind old sun will know.

Think how it wakes the seeds, –
Woke, once, the clays of a cold star.
Are limbs, so dear-achieved, are sides, 10
Full-nerved, – still warm, – too hard to stir?
Was it for this the clay grew tall?
– O what made fatuous sunbeams toil
To break earth's sleep at all?

WILFRED OWEN
(1893–1918)

Futility – Pointlessness
6 *rouse* – wake
10 *so dear-achieved* – made at such cost
13 *fatuous* – stupid

Activities

Discussion and notemaking

In groups, discuss these questions, make notes, then share your ideas in a class discussion.

1. Why does the speaker suggest moving the body into the sun? What does he say about how the sun used to affect the soldier (lines 2–5)?
2. In lines 6–7 what does the speaker say about the sun and how it might affect him now?
3. In lines 8–9 why does the speaker reflect on the sun as a life-giving force?
4. Talk about the three questions that are asked in lines 10–14. Discuss each one in turn and say how it expresses the person's increasing despair at the soldier's death.

Speaking and listening

❧ In groups, hotseat the speaker in front of a group of reporters who question him about the views he expresses in the poem. First, draw up a list of questions to ask the speaker, then act out the questioning, making notes of his replies. Discuss what he said, then in pairs draft a short item for either a television or radio report based on his answers. Compare your reports in a class discussion.

❧ In pairs, discuss the changes of tone between the two verses and how the poem gradually builds towards a cry of despair at the futility of life. Rehearse reading the poem aloud, then take it in turns to present your readings to the rest of the class. Decide which readings most effectively show the change of tone and convey the speaker's reflections on the soldier's death.

Writing

❧ Before he died, Owen had begun to draft a Preface for a book of his poems:

> This book is not about heroes. English Poetry is not yet fit to speak of them.
> Nor is it about deeds, or lands, nor anything about glory, honour, might, majesty, dominion, or power, except War.
> Above all I am not concerned with Poetry.
> My subject is War, and the pity of War.
> The Poetry is in the pity.
> Yet these elegies are to this generation in no sense consolatory. They may be to the next. All a poet can do today is warn.

Discuss how in his poems 'Disabled' and 'Futility' Owen conveys 'the pity of War'.

The Lament of the Demobilised

About the poet

Vera Brittain (1893–1970) is famous for *Testament of Youth*, an autobiographical account of what the First World War meant to the young men and women of her generation. Her experiences of its horrors – both her brother and her fiancé were killed – converted her 'from an ordinary patriotic young woman into a convinced pacifist'. Throughout her life she played a prominent part in feminist and pacifist campaigns. She attracted considerable hostility during the Second World War by her public protests at the saturation bombing of Germany.

About the poem

At the start of the First World War, Vera Brittain was a student at Oxford University. But in 1915, she gave up her studies to become a VAD (Voluntary Aid Detachment) nurse. She went first to Malta, then France. In the poem, she writes about the attitude of people who stayed at home to the young soldiers returning from the war, and about the thoughts and feelings of the returning soldiers.

The Lament of the Demobilised

'Four years,' some say consolingly. 'Oh well,
What's that? You're young. And then it must have been
A very fine experience for you!'
And they forget
How others stayed behind and just got on – 5
Got on the better since we were away.
And we came home and found
They had achieved, and men revered their names,
But never mentioned ours;
And no one talked heroics now, and we 10
Must just go back and start again once more.
'You threw four years into the melting-pot –
Did you indeed!' these others cry. 'Oh well,
The more fool you!'
And we're beginning to agree with them. 15

VERA BRITTAIN
(1893–1970)

Demobilised – soldiers released from army
8 *revered* – honoured

Activities

Discussion and notemaking

In pairs discuss these questions, make notes, and then share your ideas in a class discussion.

1. In lines 1–3 what do people who did not fight say in order to offer consolation to the returning soldiers for having given up four years of their lives to fight?
2. Why don't these words help them to feel better? Why are they not effective? (lines 4–9)
3. What does line 10 tell you about how people's attitudes to the young men who fought have changed now that the war is over?
4. What does line 11 tell you that the returning soldiers will have to do?
5. Discuss lines 12–15. What is the attitude of those who stayed behind to the people who went and fought? What effect does this attitude have on the returning soldiers?
6. Which of the words from the list below do you think best sum up how the soldiers feel on returning to civilian life after having given up four years of their lives to fight? Give reasons for your choice and suggest any other words that you think describe their feelings.
   - bitter
   - proud
   - angry
   - foolish
   - resentful
   - betrayed
   - unappreciated

Speaking and listening

❧ As a class act out a live television debate in which some demobilised soldiers and some people who stayed behind express their different views. Choose someone to act as the television presenter who will introduce the debate, ask the ex-soldiers and the civilians to express their opinions, and chair the follow-up discussion with contributions from the audience.

Writing

❧ Use what you have learned from the poem about the thoughts and feelings of returning soldiers to write a diary entry that a demobilised soldier might have written.

There will come soft rains

About the poet

Sara Teasdale (1884–1933) was an American poet, born in St Louis, who died at the age of 49 from an overdose of barbiturates. Her poetry was influenced by the work of Christina Rossetti (see page 7). She would draft and redraft her poems many times before she was satisfied with them, believing that a poet 'should try to give his poem the quiet swiftness of flame, so that the reader will feel and not think while he is reading. But the thinking will come afterwards.'

About the poem

In this poem Sara Teasdale describes a post-war world in which humanity may have destroyed itself. The poem is written in rhyming couplets, pairs of lines which rhyme.

Before you read the poem remind yourself what alliteration (see page 18) and personification (see page 28) are.

There will come soft rains

There will come soft rains and the smell of the ground,
And swallows calling with their shimmering sound;

And frogs in the pools singing at night,
And wild plum-trees in tremulous white;

Robins will wear their feathery fire 5
Whistling their whims on a low-fence wire;

And not one will know of the war, not one
Will care at last when it is done.

Not one would mind, neither bird nor tree,
If mankind perished utterly; 10

And Spring herself, when she woke at dawn,
Would scarcely know that we were gone.

SARA TEASDALE
(1884–1933)

6 *whims* – i.e. as they please

Activities

Discussion and notemaking

In groups discuss these questions, make notes, then share your ideas in a class discussion.

1. List the details of the post-war springtime scene that Sara Teasdale describes in lines 1–6. What impression of the scene is created by the sights, sounds and smells she describes?
2. Discuss Sara Teasdale's choice of **adjectives** in lines 1–6. What kind of world is suggested by
   - 'soft' (line 1)
   - 'shimmering' (line 2)
   - 'wild' (line 3)
   - 'tremulous' (line 3)
   - 'feathery' (line 5)?
3. Discuss the use she makes of alliteration in lines 1–6. How does her use of alliteration contribute to the scene she is describing in these lines?
4. In lines 7–12 what does Sara Teasdale suggest will be the effect of humanity destroying itself? Which of the three couplets do you think most effectively expresses her view?
5. Discuss how she uses repetition in lines 7–10 to make her statement more powerful.
6. Discuss the use she makes of **adverbs** in lines 10 and 12. What is the effect of her choice of 'utterly' (line 10) and 'scarcely' (line 12)?
7. Explain how she uses the personification of Spring in lines 11 and 12 to highlight the absence of human life and to suggest that its absence is insignificant.

Speaking and listening

❧ In pairs, prepare a reading of the poem. Experiment with different ways of dividing up the poem between two voices in order to discover the most effective way of putting the poet's message across. Then, present your readings to the rest of the class. Discuss which readings are the most effective and why.

Writing

❧ 'Sara Teasdale's poem left me feeling profoundly depressed.'
'Sara Teasdale's poem is a potent protest against war.'

Discuss these two views of 'There will come soft rains'. State how you felt after reading the poem, and explain how Sara Teasdale imagines a post-war world from which humanity has disappeared to convey her feelings about the consequences of war.

General Questions

Before you begin answering a question, read each of the poems you are considering writing about. Look at the notes you made when you studied the poem previously, and then read the poem again. Then check that you

- understand what the poem means;
- can say something about your response to a) its tone, b) its language, c) its imagery, and d) its verse form;
- have made up your mind about how the poem affects you;
- are ready to support or argue with the poem's theme.

If necessary, use the Glossary to check the meaning of any technical terms that you want to use when writing about the poems.

1. The First World War changed the way that some people thought about war and patriotism. Describe and compare the different attitudes to war shown by Brooke and Macaulay with those shown by Owen and Sassoon.
2. Several of the poems describe the actual suffering in war. Comment on the way that people's suffering is portrayed in 'Disabled', 'Ambulance Train' and 'Suicide'. Say which poem you find most effective and why.
3. Re-read 'Futility'. Drawing on your response to that poem, and any others you may wish to refer to, argue either that the practice of war is or is not justified.
4. Some poets write to gain the sympathy of their readers, others to shock them. Choose *two* poems in each category and write about them, commenting on their effectiveness.
5. In which of the poems do you think the author has chosen a verse form which is especially suitable for the poem's subject? Chose *two or three* poems and comment on them in detail (e.g. you might like to look at 'The Destruction of Sennacherib', 'Ambulance Train', 'Lament for the Demobilised').
6. Compare how the feelings of people at home are portrayed in 'The Flowers of the Forest' and 'Suicide'.
7. In a pair, discuss which poems have most powerfully made you think about war. Then each choose one of the poems that you discussed and prepare a short talk explaining why you chose that poem.
8. From your reading of the poems in this section, what feelings do you have about the consequences of conflict? In your answer refer to at least *three* poems and explain your reactions to them.

People

The Prioress

About the poet

Geoffrey Chaucer (*c.*1343–1400) was the greatest English poet of the Middle Ages. He came from a middle-class family and worked as a government official. His most famous work is 'The Canterbury Tales', a collection of stories told by a party of pilgrims on a journey from London to Canterbury to visit the shrine of Thomas à Becket, murdered in his cathedral on 29 December 1170. Chaucer's house in Greenwich overlooked the London to Canterbury road. Seeing people making the pilgrimage might have suggested to Chaucer the idea of using the journey as a way of framing his stories, since medieval pilgrims were notorious for the tales they told.

About the poem

The description of 'The Prioress' comes from the introduction, known as 'The General Prologue', to 'The Canterbury Tales', in which Chaucer gives a portrait of each of the pilgrims, a professional and moral cross-section of society. The prioress is one of three pilgrims who were in religious orders.

Chaucer wrote in the East Midlands dialect of Middle English, used from about 1100 to 1485, from which Standard English has developed. Pronunciation has changed since Chaucer's day; the meanings of some words have changed, and others have dropped out of the language completely. The modern verse translation, by Nevill Coghill, appears opposite the original to help you understand Chaucer's words and phrases.

The Prioress

Ther was also a Nonne, a PRIORESSE,
That of hir smylyng was ful symple and coy;
Hire gretteste ooth was but by Seinte Loy;
And she was cleped madame Eglentyne.
Ful weel she soong the service dyvyne, 5
Entuned in hir nose ful semely,
And Frenssh she spak ful faire and fetisly,
After the scole of Stratford atte Bowe,
For Frenssh of Parys was to hire unknowe.
At mete wel ytaught was she with alle: 10
She leet no morsel from hir lippes falle,
Ne wette hir fyngres in hir sauce depe;
Wel koude she carie a morsel and wel kepe
That no drope ne fille upon hire brest.
In curteisie was set ful muchel hir lest. 15
Hir over-lippe wyped she so clene
That in hir coppe ther was no ferthyng sene
Of grece, whan she dronken hadde hir draughte.
Ful semely after hir mete she raughte.
And sikerly she was of greet desport, 20
And ful plesaunt, and amyable of port,
And peyned hire to countrefete cheere
Of court, and to been estatlich of manere,
And to ben holden digne of reverence.
But, for to speken of hire conscience, 25
She was so charitable and so pitous
She wolde wepe, if that she saugh a mous
Kaught in a trappe, if it were deed or bledde.
Of smale houndes hadde she that she fedde
With rosted flessh, or milk and wastel-breed. 30
But soore wepte she if oon of hem were deed,
Or if men smoot it with a yerde smerte;
And al was conscience and tendre herte.
Ful semyly hir wympul pynched was,
Hir nose tretys, hir eyen greye as glas, 35
Hir mouth ful smal, and therto softe and reed;
But sikerly she hadde a fair forheed;
It was almoost a spanne brood, I trowe;

There also was a *Nun*, a Prioress;
Simple her way of smiling was and coy.
Her greatest oath was only 'By St Loy!'
And she was known as Madam Eglantyne.
And well she sang a service, with a fine 5
Intoning through her nose, as was most seemly,
And she spoke daintily in French, extremely,
After the school of Stratford-atte-Bowe;
French in the Paris style she did not know.
At meat her manners were well taught withal; 10
No morsel from her lips did she let fall,
Nor dipped her fingers in the sauce too deep;
But she could carry a morsel up and keep
The smallest drop from falling on her breast.
For courtliness she had a special zest. 15
And she would wipe her upper lip so clean
That not a trace of grease was to be seen
Upon the cup when she had drunk; to eat,
She reached a hand sedately for the meat.
She certainly was very entertaining, 20
Pleasant and friendly in her ways, and straining
To counterfeit a courtly kind of grace,
A stately bearing fitting to her place,
And to seem dignified in all her dealings.
As for her sympathies and tender feelings, 25
She was so charitably solicitous
She used to weep if she but saw a mouse
Caught in a trap, if it were dead or bleeding.
And she had little dogs she would be feeding
With roasted flesh, or milk, or fine white bread. 30
Sorely she wept if one of them were dead
Or someone took a stick and made it smart;
She was all sentiment and tender heart.
Her veil was gathered in a seemly way,
Her nose was elegant, her eyes glass-grey; 35
Her mouth was very small, but soft and red,
And certainly she had a well-shaped head,
Almost a span across the brows, I own;

For, hardily, she was nat undergrowe.
Ful fetys was hir cloke, as I was war. 40
Of smal coral aboute hire arm she bar
A peire of bedes, gauded al with grene,
And theron heng a brooch of gold ful sheene,
On which ther was first write a crowned A,
And after *Amor vincit omnia.* 45

GEOFFREY CHAUCER
(*c.*1343–1400)

Activities

Discussion and notemaking

In pairs, read Chaucer's portrait of the prioress and use Nevill Coghill's translation to help you understand the words and phrases in Chaucer's language which are different from today's Standard English. Then, in groups, study Chaucer's original text and discuss these questions. Each keep notes of your ideas, then share them in a class discussion.

1. Lines 1–19 mainly describe the prioress's manners and behaviour; lines 20–33 her character; and lines 34–39 her appearance. In three columns, list the words and phrases which are most revealing about her.
2. Which parts of the portrait suggest that the prioress has a worldly outlook on life?
3. Discuss how the prioress wants people to see her. Which lines tell you she is concerned about the impression she creates?
4. Discuss how Chaucer suggests the prioress's shortcomings by his use of **irony** (lines 7–9, 25–28).
5. The inscription on the prioress's brooch means 'Love conquers all', a quotation from the Latin poet, Virgil, describing human love. The medieval Church adopted it to refer to divine love, and in Chaucer's time the phrase could have either meaning. Why does the prioress wear a brooch with this inscription? What meaning or meanings does a) she b) Chaucer intend?
6. What is your final impression of the prioress? Discuss the statements below. Which, if any, sums up your opinion of her?
   - A rather worldly but gentle caring person
   - A charming hypocrite
   - A courtly lady aware of her own shortcomings
   - An amiable person, trying unsuccessfully to be both a prioress and a lady
   - An attractive personality, but rather an unsuitable prioress

She was indeed by no means undergrown.
Her cloak, I noticed, had a graceful charm. 40
She wore a coral trinket on her arm,
A set of beads, the gaudies tricked in green,
Whence hung a golden brooch of brightest sheen
On which there first was graven a crowned A,
And lower, *Amor vincit omnia.* 45

10 *meat* – a meal
10 *withal* – moreover
26 *solicitous* – concerned
34 *seemly* – suitable
38 *own* – admit
42 *tricked* – decorated
45 *Amor vincit omnia* – Love conquers all

7. Discuss which word(s) in this list most accurately describe Chaucer's attitude to the prioress. Can you suggest any others?

- disapproval
- admiration
- amusement
- criticism
- sympathy
- fascination
- scorn
- respect

Speaking and listening

❧ Read the descriptions of some of the other pilgrims (e.g. the knight, the miller, the poor parson) in Neville Coghill's modern translation of 'The General Prologue'. Hotseat one or two of them, and question them about the prioress. In your debriefing discuss which of them you think gave the most accurate picture of the prioress.

❧ In pairs, role play an interview with the prioress in which the interviewer asks her about aspects of her life which some people might criticise as too worldly. Take it in turns to be the prioress, and either tape-record the interviews or take notes of the prioress's replies.

Writing

❧ Using the replies from the interviews (above) write a magazine article entitled 'An interview with Madam Eglantyne'.

❧ What impression of the prioress does Chaucer give you? Explain how he creates this view of her, and say what you think Chaucer's attitude is towards her.

Thomas Shadwell

About the poet

John Dryden (1631–1700) was the foremost literary figure in the second half of the seventeenth century, writing plays, poems and critical essays, and translating Chaucer and the classics. He was appointed Poet Laureate in 1668. The Poet Laureate is appointed for life and is expected to write poems about important royal occasions, such as weddings and funerals. However, because he was a Catholic, Dryden had to give up the post in 1688 on the succession of the Protestant William III. The publication of his translation of the Latin poet Virgil in 1697 was a national event, and when he died he was buried in Westminster Abbey. Many of his poems were **satires**, aimed at exposing the vices of politicians or attacking other writers.

About the poem

These lines are an extract from a long political satire 'Absalom and Achitophel', published in 1682, which Dryden is said to have written at the request of King Charles II. Dryden was a Tory who supported the King on the key issue of the royal succession. He used the poem to attack the Whigs, who were opposed to the succession of James, Duke of York, because he was a Catholic. Here Dryden presents a satirical portrait of Thomas Shadwell, a fellow writer and a Whig, who subsequently succeeded Dryden as Poet Laureate in 1688.

Thomas Shadwell

Now stop your noses, readers, all and some,
For here's a tun of midnight work to come,
Og, from a treason-tavern rolling home.
Round as a globe, and liquored ev'ry chink,
Goodly and great he sails behind his link. 5
With all this bulk there's nothing lost in Og,
For ev'ry inch that is not fool is rogue:
A monstrous mass of foul corrupted matter,
As all the devils had spewed to make the batter.
When wine has given him courage to blaspheme, 10
He curses God, but God before cursed him;
And if man could have reason, none has more,
That made his paunch so rich and him so poor.
But though Heav'n made him poor, (with rev'rence speaking,)
He never was a poet of God's making. 15
The midwife laid her hand on his thick skull,
With this prophetic blessing: *Be thou dull*;
Drink, swear, and roar, forbear no lewd delight
Fit for thy bulk, do anything but write.

John Dryden
(1631–1700)

1 *stop* – block
2 *tun* – large cask
5 *link* – torch
13 *paunch* – belly
18 *forbear* – abstain from
18 *lewd* – debauched

Activities

Discussion and notemaking

In pairs, discuss these questions. Each make notes of your ideas, then share them in a group or class discussion.

1. What does Dryden suggest about Shadwell by calling him 'a tun of midnight work', and nicknaming him Og (lines 2, 3)?
2. What do you learn about Og's appearance and behaviour in lines 1–5? What does Og feel about himself, and what does Dryden make you feel about him?
3. What further details does Dryden give about Og in lines 6–9? How do they alter your feelings about him?

4. Discuss lines 10–13. What do they tell you about Og's character? What do they suggest he would be like as a) a friend b) an enemy?

5. Discuss what lines 14–17 suggest about Shadwell's writing. In the final couplet, how does Dryden reinforce his feelings about Shadwell as a writer?

6. How does Dryden make you feel towards Shadwell? *Either* choose the word(s) from this list which sum up your feelings *or* suggest others of your own.

   - amused
   - offended
   - admiring
   - afraid
   - repelled
   - contemptuous
   - sympathetic

Speaking and listening

❧ Role play a conversation between two people with different reactions to the poem. One admires it and finds it amusing, the other thinks it cruel and offensive. Present your role plays to the rest of the class and discuss the reasons why some people find the poem amusing and others find it cruel and offensive.

Writing

❧ What impression does Dryden's portrait of Og give of Thomas Shadwell? Explain how Dryden creates this picture, commenting on the language, tone and form of the poem, as well as the features of Shadwell's character that he attacks.

George Villiers

About the poet

Alexander Pope (1688–1744) was born into a Catholic family and educated mainly at home, because during the late seventeenth century Catholics were not allowed to attend Protestant universities. He suffered from ill-health throughout his life and as a result of a childhood illness, which left him with a curved spine, he never grew more than 4 feet 6 inches tall. Pope often used his poems to poke fun at fashionable society or present arguments about its morals. He was famous for short, witty statements, often ridiculing human weaknesses – for example, 'A little learning is a dangerous thing'.

About the poem

This portrait comes from Pope's third 'Moral Essay', a poem entitled 'Of the Use of Riches'. It draws lessons about human nature from the way people use wealth.

George Villiers was the second Duke of Buckingham, and a prominent figure in the court of Charles II. Pope bases his portrait on a legend which, though not historically accurate, grew up after Villiers' death. In a note on the poem Pope wrote: 'This Lord, yet more famous for his vices than his misfortunes, after having been possess'd of about £50,000 a year, and passed thro' many of the highest posts in the kingdom, died in the year 1687, in a remote inn in Yorkshire, reduc'd to the utmost misery.'

The poem is written in **heroic couplets**.

George Villiers

Behold what blessings Wealth to life can lend!
And see, what comfort it affords our end.
In the worst inn's worst room, with mat half-hung,
The floors of plaster, and the wall of dung,
On once a flock-bed, but repaired with straw, 5
With tape-ty'd curtains, never meant to draw,
The George and Garter dangling from that bed
Where tawdry yellow strove with dirty red,
Great Villiers lies—alas! how chang'd from him
That life of pleasure, and that soul of whim! 10
Gallant and gay, in Cliveden's proud alcove,
The bow'r of wanton Shrewsbury and love;
Or just as gay, at Council, in a ring
Of mimick'd Statesmen, and their merry King.
No Wit to flatter, left of all his store! 15
No Fool to laugh at, which he valu'd more.
There, Victor of his health, of fortune, friends,
And fame; this lord of useless thousands ends.

Alexander Pope
(1688–1744)

1 *lend* – bestow
2 *affords our end* – provides when we die
3 *mat half-hung* – rush mat, hung to block draughts
4 *walls of dung* – dung was used in plaster between bare laths
5 *flock-bed* – mattress stuffed with wool. The aristocracy normally used feather beds
7 *George and Garter* – highest decoration by King
8 *tawdry* – showy but worthless
10 *whim* – changeable impulse
11 *Cliveden's* – Buckingham's mansion on the banks of the River Thames
11 *alcove* – private retreat
12 *Shrewsbury* – Countess of Shrewsbury, Buckingham's mistress
12 *bow'r* – secluded place
12 *wanton* – promiscuous
13 *Council* – Privy Council
14 *mimick'd* – imitated and mocked

Activities

Discussion and notemaking

In pairs, discuss these questions. Each make notes of your answers, then share your ideas in a group discussion.

1. List the details you are given of the room where Villiers dies (lines 3–9). What do they tell you about his circumstances at the end of his life?
2. Which words and phrases in lines 9–14 describe the contrast with the life that he had led earlier?
3. What do lines 15–18 tell you about the kind of people he specially missed at the end of his life? What do they reveal about his character, and how his behaviour led him to die in such circumstances?
4. The first two lines provide an ironic introduction to the portrait. What 'blessings' and 'comfort' have wealth brought Villiers? What moral is Pope pointing out?

Speaking and listening

❧ In groups, study the poem's punctuation and sentence structure, and discuss how it can be used when preparing a reading of the poem. Talk about the attitude towards Villiers that you want your reading of the poem to convey and the tone of voice that you are going to adopt to put across that attitude. Then, take it in turns to read the poem aloud. Decide whose reading is the most effective and why.

Research and writing

❧ Basing your ideas on the information you are given in the poem, write the letter that Villiers might have written to a friend at court shortly before his death, describing his circumstances and reflecting on his life.
❧ Dryden (see page 90) portrayed Villiers as Zimri in his poem 'Absalom and Achitophel' (lines 544–62). Compare Dryden's portrait with Pope's, commenting on the similarities and differences. Which portrait do you find more effective? Give your reasons.

My Last Duchess

About the poet

For details about Robert Browning, see page 35.

About the poem

This poem is a dramatic monologue, a poem in which a single speaker addresses an audience. In a dramatic monologue, the poet uses what the person has to say to reveal his character to the reader – through what he talks about, the opinions he expresses, his manner of speech, and his attitude to his audience.

In 'My Last Duchess' the speaker is an Italian duke who lived at the time of the Renaissance – the period during the fourteenth, fifteenth and sixteenth centuries when there was a great revival of art, literature and learning in Europe. He is taking round his picture gallery a representative from a count whose daughter he hopes to marry, and showing him the painting of his last duchess.

The poem is written in rhyming couplets, which run on and so enable Browning effectively to capture the colloquial nature of the duke's speech.

My Last Duchess

That's my last Duchess painted on the wall,
Looking as if she were alive; I call
That piece a wonder, now: Frà Pandolf's hands
Worked busily a day, and there she stands.
Will't please you sit and look at her? I said 5
'Frà Pandolf' by design, for never read
Strangers like you that pictured countenance,
The depth and passion of its earnest glance,
But to myself they turned (since none puts by
The curtain I have drawn for you, but I) 10
And seemed as they would ask me, if they durst,
How such a glance came there; so, not the first
Are you to turn and ask thus. Sir, 'twas not
Her husband's presence only, called that spot
Of joy into the Duchess' cheek: perhaps 15
Frà Pandolf chanced to say 'Her mantle laps
Over my Lady's wrist too much,' or 'Paint
Must never hope to reproduce the faint
Half-flush that dies along her throat;' such stuff
Was courtesy, she thought, and cause enough 20
For calling up that spot of joy. She had
A heart … how shall I say? … too soon made glad,

Too easily impressed; she liked whate'er
She looked on, and her looks went everywhere.
Sir, 'twas all one! My favour at her breast, 25
The dropping of the daylight in the West,
The bough of cherries some officious fool
Broke in the orchard for her, the white mule
She rode with round the terrace – all and each
Would draw from her alike the approving speech, 30
Or blush, at least. She thanked men, – good; but thanked
Somehow ... I know not how ... as if she ranked
My gift of a nine hundred years old name
With anybody's gift. Who'd stoop to blame
This sort of trifling? Even had you skill 35
In speech – (which I have not) – to make your will
Quite clear to such an one, and say, 'Just this
Or that in you disgusts me; here you miss,
Or there exceed the mark' – and if she let
Herself be lessoned so, nor plainly set 40
Her wits to yours, forsooth, and made excuse,
– E'en then would be some stooping and I chuse
Never to stoop. Oh Sir, she smiled, no doubt,
Whene'er I passed her; but who passed without
Much the same smile? This grew; I gave commands; 45
Then all smiles stopped together. There she stands
As if alive. Will't please you rise? We'll meet
The company below, then. I repeat,
The Count your Master's known munificence
Is ample warrant that no just pretence 50
Of mine for dowry will be disallowed;
Though his fair daughter's self, as I avowed
At starting, is my object. Nay, we'll go
Together down, Sir! Notice Neptune, tho'
Taming a sea-horse, thought a rarity, 55
Which Claus of Innsbruck cast in bronze for me.

ROBERT BROWNING
(1812–89)

3 *Frà* – title given to Italian friar
7 *countenance* – face
9 *puts by* – pulls back
11 *durst* – dared
16 *mantle laps* – cloak falls
20 *courtesy* – code of good manners
25 *favour* – love token
27 *officious* – over-keen to please
33 *name* – i.e. his family name
39 *exceed the mark* – go beyond what's suitable
40 *plainly set Her wits to yours* – argued with you
49 *munificence* – generosity
50 *ample warrant* – sufficient guarantee
50 *just pretence* – rightful claim
52 *avowed* – admitted

Activities

Discussion and notemaking

Read through the poem twice on your own. What are your first impressions of the duke and his portrayal of his last duchess? Note down your ideas in two columns, and then discuss them with a partner. Together answer the following questions, then share your views in either a group or a class discussion.

1. What does the duke say in lines 5–12 about how people react to seeing the duchess's picture? Why does he say 'Frà Pandolf' intentionally (line 6)?
2. What is implied by the statement he makes in the brackets in lines 9 and 10?
3. What do you learn in lines 5–21 about the expression on the duchess's face ? What did her 'glance' look like? What is her 'spot of joy', and what caused it?
4. What do lines 21–31 tell you about the duchess's behaviour and about her temperament and character? What do these lines tell you about the duke and his view of her? Is he right to be critical of her?
5. Why does the duke talk about his name (line 33)? What does he reveal in lines 31–33 about himself and his attitude to the duchess?
6. What does the duke say he would not stoop to do (lines 34–43)? What does his refusal to stoop (lines 42–43) tell you about the duke's character and his feelings towards the duchess?
7. What does the duke say in lines 43–45 about the duchess's smiling? What were the commands he gave (line 45)? Why did he give them?
8. What does the duke reveal about himself by the way he closes the subject of his last duchess and starts to discuss business (lines 47–53)? What does he emphasise (lines 48–51), and what does this tell you about him?
9. What does he add in lines 52–53 which suggests he thinks he may have over-emphasised the business side of the proposed marriage? Discuss how the phrase 'my object' can be interpreted.
10. What is the duke's final comment before he leaves the gallery? What does this tell you about him?

11. Look back at the notes you made on your first impressions of the duke. What is your final impression of him? Study the list of words below and choose those five which you think best sum up the duke's character. Can you suggest any others? Find evidence from the poem to support your views.

    - haughty
    - selfish
    - cunning
    - materialistic
    - arrogant
    - proud
    - malevolent
    - shrewd
    - cynical
    - sensitive
    - callous
    - aloof
    - possessive
    - reticent
    - unscrupulous

12. What is your final impression of the duchess? Do you think she herself was in any way responsible for her own fate? Make a list of words which sum up your impression of her character.

Speaking and listening

❧ Role play a scene in which the envoy returns home and tells a friend about his meeting with the duke and his impression of the duke. Choose some pairs to present their role plays to the rest of the class, and discuss what each of the envoys says about the duke.

❧ Imagine that the duke is showing a group of reporters round his picture gallery. In groups, role play the scene, then hold a class discussion during which you hotseat the people who role played the duke. Finally, discuss what you have learned from this activity about the duke's character and the impression he is trying to give of his last duchess.

Writing

❧ In pairs, plan how you would produce a film to accompany a reading of the poem. In your film script, give full details of the pictures you would show at each point in the poem. Include notes explaining what the picture gallery would be like, and how the characters would be dressed.

❧ Write a letter that the duchess might have written to a confidante shortly after Frà Pandolf had finished painting her portrait describing her feelings about the picture, her husband's reaction to it, and her feelings about the way he is behaving towards her.

❧ Explain how in 'My Last Duchess' Browning uses the form of a dramatic monologue to create not only the character of the duke but also of the duchess.

Proud Maisie

About the poet

Sir Walter Scott (1771–1832) was a Scottish writer, famous for his novels, such as *Ivanhoe*. He grew up in the Scottish Borders and as a child caught polio which left him lame. He went to Edinburgh University and then worked as a lawyer. He was interested in old Border tales and ballads and was well-known for his poetry before he turned to writing novels. Although his novels were very popular, Scott got into financial trouble and spent the last years of his life working at a frantic pace in an attempt to pay off his debts. On his death, they were cleared by the sale of his copyrights.

About the poem

This poem is a literary ballad. At the end of the eighteenth and beginning of the nineteenth century, poets such as Wordsworth (see page 101), Coleridge (see page 124) and Keats (see page 127) chose the traditional ballad form for some of the poems they wrote about people and events. Such poems are known as literary ballads.

'Proud Maisie' is from chapter 40 of Scott's novel *The Heart of Midlothian*. It is sung on her death-bed by one of the characters, Madge Wildfire.

Proud Maisie is in the wood

Proud Maisie is in the wood,
   Walking so early;
Sweet Robin sits on the bush,
   Singing so rarely.

'Tell me, thou bonny bird,   5
When shall I marry me?'
'When six braw gentlemen
Kirkward shall carry ye.'

'Who makes the bridal bed,
Birdie, say truly?'   10
'The grey-headed sexton
That delves the grave duly.

'The glow-worm o'er grave and stone
Shall light thee steady;
The owl from the steeple sing,   15
"Welcome, proud lady."'

Sir Walter Scott
(1771–1832)

7 *braw* – fine   8 *kirkward* – church-wards   12 *delves* – digs

Activities

Discussion and notemaking

In pairs, discuss these questions, make notes, then share your ideas in a group discussion.

1. What scene is described in the first verse? What mood is created by the first six lines of the poem?
2. What do lines 7 and 8 tell you about how Maisie imagines her future? Discuss how Scott uses images of death in verses 2, 3 and 4 to provide a contrast with images of a young woman going to church to get married.
3. Which of these words best describe the mood that Scott creates in this poem?
   - sadness
   - depression
   - grief
   - acceptance
   - melancholy
   - foreboding
   - despair
   - sorrow
   - inevitability

Can you suggest any others?

Speaking and listening

❧ In groups, rehearse a reading of the poem to present to the rest of the class. Decide what impression you want your reading to create. Then, experiment with dividing up the poem between different voices in order to create that impression. Discuss which reading was most effective and why.

The Solitary Reaper

About the poet

William Wordsworth (1770–1850) and his poetry are associated with the Lake District, where he grew up and lived most of his life. Many of his best poems were written while he was living with his sister Dorothy at Dove Cottage in Grasmere. He was Poet Laureate from 1843 to 1850. His best-known poems include a long autobiographical poem, 'The Prelude', and 'I wandered lonely as a cloud', a poem about the impression made on him by seeing daffodils growing in Gowbarrow Park, near Ullswater.

About the poem

During a walking tour of Scotland in the autumn of 1803, Wordsworth and his sister Dorothy (who kept a journal about their travels) stayed with Burns (see page 39) and Scott (see page 99). Though grateful for the kindness of the ordinary people, they were struck by the harsh climate and barren landscape, as well as the poverty among the peasantry, few of whom spoke English. During a second visit two years later, Wordsworth wrote Scottish poems which drew on memories of his previous visit. He again saw people working in the fields, isolated against the immense Highland landscape. But the direct stimulus for 'The Solitary Reaper' was this passage in Thomas Wilkinson's *Tours to the British Mountains*: 'Passed a female who was reaping alone; she sung in Erse as she bended over her sickle; the sweetest human voice I ever heard: her strains were tenderly melancholy, and felt delicious, long after they were heard no more.'

The Solitary Reaper

Behold her, single in the field,
Yon solitary Highland Lass!
Reaping and singing by herself;
Stop here, or gently pass!
Alone she cuts and binds the grain, 5
And sings a melancholy strain;
O listen! for the Vale profound
Is overflowing with the sound.

No Nightingale did ever chaunt
More welcome notes to weary bands 10
Of travellers in some shady haunt,
Among Arabian sands:
A voice so thrilling ne'er was heard
In spring-time from the Cuckoo-bird,
Breaking the silence of the seas 15
Among the farthest Hebrides.

Will no one tell me what she sings? –
Perhaps the plaintive numbers flow
For old, unhappy, far-off things,
And battles long ago: 20
Or is it some more humble lay,
Familiar matter of to-day?
Some natural sorrow, loss, or pain,
That has been, and may be again?

Whate'er the theme, the Maiden sang 25
As if her song could have no ending;
I saw her singing at her work,
And o'er the sickle bending: –
I listened, motionless and still;
And, as I mounted up the hill, 30
The music in my heart I bore,
Long after it was heard no more.

WILLIAM WORDSWORTH
(1770–1850)

7 *Vale profound* – deep valley
9 *chaunt* – sing
18 *plaintive numbers* – sad words of her song
21 *lay* – song

Activities

Discussion and notemaking

On your own, read the poem and make notes in reply to these questions. Then, in groups, see if you can improve your answers. Next, use a whole class discussion to try to find agreed answers.

1. What do you learn from verse 1 which adds to what you know from the poem's title?
2. What do the comparisons in verse 2 tell you of the poet's feelings about the woman's song?
3. In verse 3, why can he not understand her song? What do his questions suggest the song may be about? What do these suggestions say about its mood?
4. What does verse 4 tell you about a) how the woman's song affected the poet b) why she is singing it?
5. List the reasons why the poet found the solitary reaper so memorable.

Speaking and listening

❧ In groups, discuss the structure of the poem. Talk about how verses 1 and 4 consist of the poet's observations and verses 2 and 3 of his reflections. Then prepare a reading of the poem which shows the contrast between the first and final verses and verses 2 and 3. Present your reading to the rest of the class, and decide which reading is the most effective and why.

Writing

❧ Write the journal entry which Dorothy Wordsworth might have made at the end of a day's walk during which they saw the reaper.

❧ Look in the art section of the library and find a painting or photograph of a person or a landscape which intrigues you. Write about it in the way that Wordsworth wrote about the reaper, including your reflections as well as your observations. Choose your own verse form (e.g. couplets, quatrains or eight-line stanzas similar to Wordsworth's).

❧ What impression does Wordsworth create of the solitary reaper? Do you think he is effective in describing both the reaper and his personal feelings about her? Give reasons for your answer.

Satan

About the poet

John Milton (1608–74) was the son of a wealthy businessman. After attending Cambridge University he retired to his father's estate in Buckinghamshire to concentrate on developing his career as a poet. His life was changed when the Civil War broke out in 1639 and he settled in London, writing a series of religious, social and political pamphlets supporting the Parliamentary cause. In 1649 he was given a senior governmental post, but had to resign when he went blind in 1652. However, he continued to write, dictating to his daughters or a secretary. His most famous poem is 'Paradise Lost', an epic poem in twelve books about the fall of Adam, which is described in the Bible in the Book of Genesis (Chapter 2 onwards).

About the poem

These lines are from Book 1 of 'Paradise Lost' which tells how Satan, having led a rebellion against God, has been thrown out of heaven and into hell. Milton described Satan with his angels as 'lying on the burning lake, thunderstruck and astonished'. Beginning to recover his senses, he addresses his second-in-command, Beelzebub.

The poem is written in **blank verse**. Milton was a classical scholar and his English style is influenced by Latin. He uses complex sentences, and often uses words in their Latin word order and original Latin meanings.

Satan

If thou beëst he; but O how fallen! how changed
From him, who in the happy realms of light
Clothed with transcendent brightness didst outshine
Myriads though bright: if he whom mutual league,
United thoughts and counsels, equal hope 5
And hazard in the glorious enterprise,
Joined with me once, now misery hath joined
In equal ruin: into what pit thou seest
From what highth fallen, so much the stronger proved
He with his thunder: and till then who knew 10
The force of those dire arms? Yet not for those,
Nor what the potent victor in his rage
Can else inflict, do I repent or change,
Though changed in outward lustre, that fixed mind
And high disdain, from sense of injured merit, 15
That with the mightiest raised me to contend,
And to the fierce contention brought along
Innumerable force of spirits armed
That durst dislike his reign, and me preferring,
His utmost power with adverse power opposed 20
In dubious battle on the plains of heaven,
And shook his throne. What though the field be lost?

All is not lost; the unconquerable will,
And study of revenge, immortal hate,
And courage never to submit or yield: 25
And what is else not to be overcome?

JOHN MILTON
(1608–74

1 *If thou beëst he* – If you really are he (Beelzebub)
2 *him* – i.e. Beelzebub
3 *transcendent* – surpassing
4 *mutual league* – common alliance
5 *counsels* – advice
8 *ruin* – fall from a great height
9 *highth* – height
10 *He* – God
11 *dire* – powerful
14 *lustre* – appearance
15 *disdain* – scorn
16 *contend* – fight
19 *durst* – dared
20 *adverse* – opposing
21 *dubious* – of uncertain result
24 *study* – pursuit of
26 *what is else … overcome* – whatever else has to be overcome

Activities

Discussion and notemaking

Discuss these questions in pairs. Each make notes of your answers, then share your ideas in a group discussion.

1. Skim through the extract and write down the words and phrases which emphasise the contrasts between heaven and hell.
2. In lines 1–4, why does Satan not recognise Beelzebub? How has he changed?
3. What does Satan say in lines 4–8 which shows how much he valued Beelzebub as his deputy?
4. What reasons does Satan give for their defeat (lines 9–11)?
5. How do lines 11–16 show that, despite the consequences, Satan does not regret having led the rebellion against God?
6. What do lines 17–22 tell you about the size of the rebel army, why Satan was chosen to lead it, and the limited success they had?
7. How does the end of the extract (lines 22–26) reveal that Satan is far from giving in, and will continue to plot against God?
8. What impression do you get of Satan from what he says and the way he speaks to Beelzebub? Discuss the changes in Satan's tone from his uncertain and hesitant beginning to the determination in the last five lines.

Speaking and listening

❧ In groups, discuss how you will mark the lines to direct an actor to speak them effectively. Consider such points as managing long phrases or sentences, pace, feeling, tone and emphasis. Explain what impression of Satan you want the actor to give. Then, take it in turns to be the actor, and decide which member of the group gives the most effective reading.

Ulysses

About the poet

Alfred, Lord Tennyson (1809–92) was one of 11 children. He started to write poetry as a child and published his first book of poems when he was at Cambridge University. In 1833, he was so deeply affected by the sudden death of a close friend, Arthur Hallam, that though he continued to write he vowed not to publish any more poetry for ten years. In the 1840s he again started to publish his poems and in 1850, on the death of William Wordsworth (see page 101), he became Poet Laureate. The appointment made him feel financially secure and he finally married Emily Smallwood, after having been engaged to her for seven years. Eventually he became so famous that people would wait outside his house hoping to catch sight of him going in or coming out. In 1884 he was made a peer. Among his most famous poems are 'The Lady of Shalott' and 'The Charge of the Light Brigade'.

About the poem

The poem takes the form of a dramatic monologue spoken by Ulysses (the Latin name for the Greek hero Odysseus), whose wanderings and exploits fighting against the Trojans are described by Homer in his epic poem 'The Odyssey'. Partly based on a passage from 'The Odyssey', this poem shows Ulysses in his last years addressing the comrades who are about to accompany him on another voyage.

The poem is in blank verse. It was written in October 1833, shortly after Hallam's death. 'It gives the feeling,' wrote Tennyson, 'about the need of going forward and braving the struggle of life.'

Ulysses

It little profits that an idle king,
By this still hearth, among these barren crags,
Matched with an agèd wife, I mete and dole
Unequal laws unto a savage race,
That hoard, and sleep, and feed, and know not me. 5

I cannot rest from travel: I will drink
Life to the lees: all times I have enjoyed
Greatly, have suffered greatly, both with those
That loved me, and alone; on shore, and when
Through scudding drifts the rainy Hyades 10
Vext the dim sea: I am become a name;
For always roaming with a hungry heart
Much have I seen and known; cities of men
And manners, climates, councils, governments,
Myself not least, but honoured of them all; 15
And drunk delight of battle with my peers,
Far on the ringing plains of windy Troy.

I am a part of all that I have met;
Yet all experience is an arch wherethrough
Gleams that untravelled world, whose margin fades 20
For ever and for ever when I move.
How dull it is to pause, to make an end,
To rust unburnished, not to shine in use!
As though to breathe were life. Life piled on life
Were all too little, and of one to me 25
Little remains: but every hour is saved
From that eternal silence, something more,
A bringer of new things; and vile it were
For some three suns to store and hoard myself,
And this gray spirit yearning in desire 30
To follow knowledge like a sinking star,
Beyond the utmost bound of human thought.

This is my son, mine own Telemachus,
To whom I leave the sceptre and the isle –
Well-loved of me, discerning to fulfil 35
This labour, by slow prudence to make mild
A rugged people, and through soft degrees
Subdue them to the useful and the good.
Most blameless is he, centred in the sphere
Of common duties, decent not to fail 40
In offices of tenderness, and pay
Meet adoration to my household gods,
When I am gone. He works his work, I mine.

There lies the port; the vessel puffs her sail:
There gloom the dark broad seas. My mariners, 45
Souls that have toiled, and wrought, and thought with me–
That ever with a frolic welcome took
The thunder and the sunshine, and opposed
Free hearts, free foreheads–you and I are old;
Old age hath yet his honour and his toil; 50

Death closes all: but something ere the end,
Some work of noble note, may yet be done,
Not unbecoming men that strove with Gods.
The lights begin to twinkle from the rocks:
The long day wanes: the slow moon climbs: the deep 55
Moans round with many voices. Come, my friends,
'Tis not too late to seek a newer world.
Push off, and sitting well in order smite
The sounding furrows; for my purpose holds
To sail beyond the sunset, and the baths 60
Of all the western stars, until I die.
It may be that the gulfs will wash us down:
It may be we shall touch the Happy Isles,
And see the great Achilles, whom we knew.
Though much is taken, much abides; and though 65
We are not now that strength which in old days
Moved earth and heaven; that which we are, we are;
One equal temper of heroic hearts,
Made weak by time and fate, but strong in will
To strive, to seek, to find, and not to yield. 70

Alfred, Lord Tennyson
(1809–92)

1 *It little profits* – It's no use
3 *mete and dole* – decide and enforce
7 *lees* – dregs
10 *Hyades* – group of stars
23 *unburnished* – unpolished, i.e. not used
30 *yearning* – longing
34 *sceptre* – royal succession
36 *make mild* – civilise
42 *Meet* – suitable
55 *wanes* – declines
55 *deep* – ocean
58 *smite … furrows* – set off through the waves
62 *gulfs* – great waves
65 *abides* – remains
68 *temper* – determination

Activities

Discussion and notemaking

In this poem Tennyson traces Ulysses' thoughts and emotions as he reflects on life and explains his decision to make another voyage. On your own, study the poem and draw a flow chart to show the development of Ulysses' thoughts and feelings through the poem. Then form groups, compare your flow charts, and discuss these questions. Make notes of your ideas and share them in a class discussion.

Section 1 (lines 1–5)

1. What do these lines tell you about Ulysses' situation and how he feels about it?

Section 2 (lines 6–17)

2. What do lines 6 and 7 tell you about Ulysses' nature and his attitude to life? What does he say in the rest of the section about how he has spent his life?

3. What are his feelings about what he has done? How would you describe his mood as he has these thoughts?

Section 3 (18–32)

4. What do these lines tell you about why Ulysses has decided to make another voyage? Pick out the words and phrases which convey the idea a) that travel would be fulfilling b) that not to travel would be a waste?

5. Discuss how Ulysses' mood begins to change as he talks about his reasons for taking up travelling again.

Section 4 (lines 33–43)

6. What does Ulysses say about his son Telemachus? How does he feel about leaving him in charge while he is away?

Section 5 (lines 44–53)

7. What does Ulysses say in these lines about the sailors who are to accompany him? What does he say to them about what he hopes the voyage will accomplish (lines 50–53)?

Section 6 (lines 54–70)

8. Discuss the description of the time of their departure that is given in lines 54–56. How is the theme of lateness developed in the rest of this section?

9. What does Ulysses say in lines 58–70 and how does it show his determination?

Speaking and listening

❧ On your own, go through the poem section by section and suggest a title for each of the sections, then form groups and compare your suggestions.

❧ In pairs, talk about how Ulysses' mood changes through the poem and think about what effect he wants each part of his speech to have on his audience. Each practise reading the poem aloud, then take it in turns to present your reading. Discuss whose reading works best and why.

❧ Imagine that you are two of the sailors who heard Ulysses' speech. One was impressed, the other unimpressed. Role play a scene in which you discuss what he said and your different reactions to it.

Writing

❧ You are a reporter for the *Ithaca Times* who listened to Ulysses' speech. Either write a newspaper report of the speech or an editorial commenting on it.

❧ Tennyson wrote about 'Ulysses': 'It gives the feeling about the need of going forward and braving the struggle of life.' Discuss how Tennyson uses the story of Ulysses as a way of expressing his thoughts and feelings following the death of a close friend.

The Slave Mother

About the poet

Frances E. W. Harper (1825–1911) was a black American poet who also wrote the first novel by an Afro-American to be published in the USA. Born to free parents, at a time when most black people in America were still slaves, she was orphaned at an early age. She was brought up by relatives who were active in the anti-slavery movement, and after working at various jobs she became a lecturer renowned for her speeches in support of women's rights and the abolition of slavery. Dramatic readings of her own poems were a highlight of her lectures.

About the poem

In this poem Frances Harper describes the anguish of a slave mother as her son is taken from her. She uses a traditonal verse form, common in ballads, of four-line verses with a regular iambic metre and the rhyme scheme abcb.

Before you read the poem, remind yourself what a metaphor is (see page 7).

The Slave Mother

Heard you that shriek? It rose
So wildly on the air,
It seem'd as if a burden'd heart
Was breaking in despair.

Saw you those hands so sadly clasped – 5
The bowed and feeble head –
The shuddering of that fragile form –
That look of grief and dread?

Saw you the sad, imploring eye?
Its every glance was pain, 10
As if a storm of agony
Were sweeping through the brain.

She is a mother pale with fear,
Her boy clings to her side,
And in her kyrtle vainly tries 15
His trembling form to hide.

He is not hers, although she bore
For him a mother's pains;
He is not hers, although her blood
Is coursing through his veins! 20

He is not hers, for cruel hands
May rudely tear apart
The only wreath of household love
That binds her breaking heart.

His love has been a joyous light 25
That o'er her pathway smiled,
A fountain gushing ever new,
Amid life's desert wild.

His lightest word has been a tone
Of music round her heart, 30
Their lives a streamlet blent in one –
Oh, Father! must they part?

They tear him from her circling arms,
Her last and fond embrace:–
Oh! never more may her sad eyes 35
Gaze on his mournful face.

No marvel, then, those bitter shrieks
Disturb the listening air;
She is a mother, and her heart
Is breaking in despair. 40

FRANCES ELLEN WATKINS HARPER
(1825–1911)

9 *imploring* – begging for help
15 *kyrtle* – gown
23 *wreath* – memorial (metaphor)
31 *blent* – mixed together

Activities

Discussion and notemaking

Discuss these questions in groups, each make notes of your ideas, then share them in a class discussion.

1. In the first verse, how does the poet convey the mother's anguish?
2. List the features of the mother's appearance that are described in verses 2 and 3. What do each tell you about her feelings? How does the metaphor in lines 11 and 12 help to stress the depth of her emotions?
3. Why is the mother 'pale with fear' (line 13)? Which words and phrases in verse 4 tell you that the boy is also afraid?
4. What does the poet tell you in verses 5 and 6 that helps to explain the mother's feelings? Whose are the 'cruel hands' (line 21)? What is 'the only wreath of household love' (line 23)? What is the effect of repeating the **paradox** 'He is not hers'?
5. What four metaphors does the poet use in verses 7 and 8 to describe the happiness that the relationship with her son has brought to the mother's life? Which of them do you find the most effective? Give your reasons.
6. What scene is described in verse 9? Pick out the words and phrases which bring out the significance of the moment.
7. How does the final verse echo the first verse? Discuss how it is different from the first verse, and how the poet uses it to make a powerful concluding statement.

Speaking and listening

❧ In pairs, produce an item for a television news broadcast in which a reporter who has witnessed the slave mother being separated from her son gives an eye-witness account of the scene and then interviews the mother. Take it in turns to present your news reports, and discuss which one most effectively conveys the mother's feelings.

Writing

❧ Write the diary entry that the slave mother may have written on the day that her son was taken from her.

❧ Discuss how in 'The Slave Mother' Frances E. W. Harper develops a poem in order to present a powerful statement against slavery.

The Song of the Shirt

About the poet

The son of a London bookseller, Thomas Hood (1799–1845) became a journalist, editing and contributing to a range of magazines including *Punch*. He wrote both comic and serious verse, but is remembered largely for his humorous poems and his skilled wordplay. *Punch* nicknamed him 'Professor of Punmanship', a title which upset him.

About the poem

This poem was inspired by an article which appeared in *Punch* on 4 November 1843 called 'Famine and fashion', which disclosed that a woman employed to make trousers received sevenpence a pair, i.e. seven shillings for a 98-hour week. The article moved Hood so much that he wrote the poem at one sitting, and it was published in the *Punch* 1843 Christmas edition. It moved ordinary people, was printed on broadsheets and handkerchiefs, recited at public gatherings and read from pulpits. It was translated into several European languages, and widely inspired poetry of social consciousness. Except for its first and last verses, the poem consists of the song Hood imagines the woman singing.

The Song of the Shirt

With fingers weary and worn,
  With eyelids heavy and red,
A woman sat, in unwomanly rags,
  Plying her needle and thread –
Stitch! stitch! stitch! 5
  In poverty, hunger, and dirt,
And still with a voice of dolorous pitch
  She sang the 'Song of the Shirt.'

'Work! work! work!
  While the cock is crowing aloof! 10
And work – work – work,
  Till the stars shine through the roof!
It's Oh! to be a slave
  Along with the barbarous Turk,
Where woman has never a soul to save, 15
  If this is Christian work.

'Work – work – work,
Till the brain begins to swim;
Work – work – work,
Till the eyes are heavy and dim! 20
Seam, and gusset, and band,
Band, and gusset, and seam,
Till over the buttons I fall asleep,
And sew them on in a dream!

'Oh, Men, with Sisters dear! 25
Oh, Men, with Mothers and Wives!
It is not linen you're wearing out
But human creatures' lives!
Stitch – stitch – stitch,
In poverty, hunger, and dirt, 30
Sewing at once, with a double thread,
A Shroud as well as a Shirt.

'But why do I talk of Death?
That Phantom of grisly bone,
I hardly fear its terrible shape, 35
It seems so like my own –
It seems so like my own,
Because of the fasts I keep;
Oh, God, that bread should be so dear,
And flesh and blood so cheap! 40

'Work – work – work!
My labour never flags;
And what are its wages? A bed of straw,
A crust of bread – and rags.
That shattered roof – this naked floor – 45
A table – a broken chair –
And a wall so blank, my shadow I thank
For sometimes falling there!

'Work – work – work!
From weary chime to chime, 50
Work – work – work,
As prisoners work for crime!
Band, and gusset, and seam,
Seam, and gusset, and band,
Till the heart is sick, and the brain benumbed, 55
As well as the weary hand.

'Work – work – work!
In the dull December light,
And work – work – work,
When the weather is warm and bright – 60
While underneath the eaves
The brooding swallows cling
As if to show me their sunny backs
And twit me with the spring.

'Oh! but to breathe the breath 65
Of the cowslip and primrose sweet –
With the sky above my head,
And the grass beneath my feet;
For only one short hour
To feel as I used to feel, 70
Before I knew the woes of want
And the walk that costs a meal.

'Oh! but for one short hour!
A respite however brief!
No blessèd leisure for Love or Hope, 75
But only time for Grief!
A little weeping would ease my heart,
But in their briny bed
My tears must stop, for every drop
Hinders needle and thread!' 80

With fingers weary and worn,
With eyelids heavy and red,
A woman sat, in unwomanly rags,
Plying her needle and thread –
Stitch! stitch! stitch! 85
In poverty, hunger, and dirt,
And still with a voice of dolorous pitch, –
Would that its tone could reach the Rich! –
She sang this 'Song of the Shirt!'

THOMAS HOOD
(1799–1845)

4 *plying* – working with
7 *dolorous* – distressed
10 *aloof* – distantly
32 *shroud* – sheet-like wrapping for corpse
42 *flags* – weakens
52 *for crime* – for committing a crime
63 *twit* – taunt
71 *want* – poverty
78 *briny* – salty

Activities

Discussion and notemaking

Study the poem on your own, reading it through at least twice. Make notes, under the following four headings, of the impressions you form of a) the woman, b) the work she has to do, c) the conditions in which she lives, and d) her attitude towards her life. Then, share your ideas in pairs and discuss these questions, each making notes of your answers.

1. Pick out the words and phrases which Hood uses in verse 1 to show that the woman is poor and that the work she does is exhausting.
2. What do verses 2 and 3 tell you about how long the woman works and the effect this has on her? Discuss the comment she makes about her work in lines 13–16. What does this suggest about the work she has to do?
3. To whom is verse 4 addressed? What does she say to them about her work (lines 27–32), and what effect does she hope this will have on them?
4. What picture of herself does the woman create in verse 5? Why has she become like this?
5. What does she say about her wages in verse 6? What picture of her room does this verse create? What do lines 47–48 tell us about how she feels about her room?
6. To whom does the woman compare herself in verse 7? How does this verse emphasise everything that the woman has said about herself and her work up to this point in the song?
7. How are images of the changing seasons used in verse 8 to provide a contrast with the unchanging nature of the woman's work?
8. What does the woman long for in verse 9? Discuss how the details of the countryside in lines 65–68 provide a contrast with those of her room (lines 43–46).
9. What is missing from the woman's life because she has to work so hard (verse 10)? What does the fact that she can't let herself cry suggest?
10. Discuss how the final verse echoes the first verse. Talk about the additional line (line 88) and what it suggests about who is to blame for the conditions of her life.
11. What is the tone of the song (line 88)? How would you describe the mood of the woman as she sings her song? Pick out the word(s) from the list below which most accurately describe her mood. Can you suggest any others? Quote evidence from the poem to support your views.

- desperation
- resignation
- defiance
- wistfulness
- hope
- sadness
- anger

Speaking and listening

❧ In groups, plan and produce an investigative television report into the conditions in which the woman lives and works. Include interviews with several women about their lives, and prepare for them by drawing up a list of questions for the interviewer to ask and discussing the answers the woman would give. Present your reports to the rest of the class, and discuss which report most effectively describes what the woman's life is like.

❧ In groups, prepare a dramatic performance of the poem, in order to convey the tone of the song and the mood of the woman as she sings it. Discuss how you could use different combinations of voices in order to show the way Hood uses rhythm and repetition to stress the monotony and repetitive nature of the woman's work. Then present your performances and discuss which parts of them were most effective.

Writing

❧ Write a newspaper editorial that might have been written in December 1843 after the poem appeared in *Punch*, commenting on the poem and the issues it raises.

Song to the Men of England

About the poet

Percy Bysshe Shelley (1792–1822) came from a wealthy family and was sent to Eton where he was bullied by the other boys, who nicknamed him 'mad Shelley' because he refused to conform. He then went to Oxford University but his outspoken views led him to be expelled. At the age of 20 he married Harriet Westbrook, but three years later left her and their two children. Harriet later committed suicide, drowning herself in the Serpentine. Shelley went to live in Italy, where he became friendly with Byron (see page 30). Shortly before his thirtieth birthday, he and a friend were drowned when their yacht capsized in a violent storm on the bay of Lerici.

About the poem

This is a political poem in which Shelley urges the mass of the population not to put up with the conditions in which they are living and working but to demand their rights. It was written during the period after the Napoleonic Wars ended in 1815, when the working classes first began to organise themselves and to make protests. Shelley believed that change must come, but that it should be gradually achieved by enlightened leadership rather than brought about by revolution.

Before reading the poem remind yourself what a metaphor is (see page 7).

Song to the Men of England

Men of England, wherefore plough
For the lords who lay ye low?
Wherefore weave with toil and care
The rich robes your tyrants wear?

Wherefore feed, and clothe, and save, 5
From the cradle to the grave,
Those ungrateful drones who would
Drain your sweat – nay, drink your blood?

Wherefore, Bees of England, forge
Many a weapon, chain and scourge, 10
That these stingless drones may spoil
The forced produce of your toil?

Have ye leisure, comfort, calm,
Shelter, food, love's gentle balm?
Or what is it ye buy so dear 15
With your pain and with your fear?

The seed ye sow, another reaps;
The wealth ye find, another keeps;
The robes ye weave, another wears;
The arms ye forge, another bears. 20

Sow seed, – but let no tyrant reap;
Find wealth, – let no imposter heap;
Weave robes, – let not the idle wear;
Forge arms, – in your defence to bear.

Shrink to your cellars, holes, and cells; 25
In halls ye deck another dwells.
Why shake the chains ye wrought? Ye see
The steel ye tempered glance on ye.

With plough and spade, and hoe and loom,
Trace your grave, and build your tomb, 30
And weave your winding-sheet, till fair
England be your sepulchre.

PERCY BYSSHE SHELLEY
(1792–1822)

1 *wherefore* – why
7 *drones* – non-working male bees (metaphor)
10 *scourge* – whip
14 *balm* – comfort
26 *deck* – decorate
28 *tempered* – hardened (metaphor)
28 *glance* – gleam
31 *winding-sheet* – shroud
32 *sepulchre* – tomb

Activities

Discussion and notemaking

Discuss these questions in groups, each making notes of your ideas, then share them in a class discussion.

1. Discuss how Shelley uses a series of questions in verses 1–4 in order to try to make people feel angry. Pick out the words and phrases he uses to suggest that working people are being exploited by unscrupulous bosses. Discuss the effect of the comparison with bees in these verses.
2. What does the question he asks in lines 13–14 suggest the workers should receive for their efforts? What do the statements in verse 5 suggest are their actual rewards?
3. Discuss how verse 6 exhorts the men of England to take action. Talk about how the commands are phrased to suggest that their deeds would be justified. How do the rhymes in this verse add to its effect by echoing the rhymes in verse 5?
4. In verses 5 – 7 how does Shelley express his scorn for the way that the men of England put up with their lot instead of taking action? Discuss how the images of death in the final verse suggest that the men are themselves responsible for the conditions in which they live their lives.
5. Discuss these statements about the poem. Which of them best sums up your own interpretation?
   - a withering attack on the way landowners and factory owners exploit their workers
   - a condemnation of the working men of England for simply putting up with being treated as sub-human
   - a plea to the men of England to rise up and demand their rights
   - an inflammatory exhortation to the men of England to rebel against injustice using force, if necessary
   - a bitter tirade railing against a situation which is unjust but about which nothing can be done

Speaking and listening

❧ As a class, act out a scene in which a worker, who shares Shelley's views, tries to convince his fellow-workers to take action, and gets into an argument with some workers who heckle him and argue that it would not do any good to rebel. Then discuss what you learned from this activity about Shelley's arguments and ideas.

Writing

❧ Use the arguments and ideas that Shelley presents in the poem and draft either a letter or a speech to try to convince 'the Men of England' that they must no longer put up with the conditions in which they are living and working.

A Poison Tree

About the poet

William Blake (1757–1827) was the son of a haberdasher and received no formal education, except training as an artist. He worked as an engraver, producing illustrations for many books, including his own books of poems. However, his books were never popular during his life and he died poor. His most famous poems are 'The Tyger' and 'Jerusalem'.

About the poem

This poem is about the harm done when anger is repressed rather than expressed. In his manuscript, Blake gave the poem the ironic title 'Christian Forbearance', because he thought that Christians tended to repress their anger. When trying to think of an image which he could engrave to illustrate the poem, Blake remembered reading about the upas tree found in Java, which has a poisonous sap.

Before you read the poem, remind yourself what a metaphor is (page 7).

A Poison Tree

I was angry with my friend:
I told my wrath, my wrath did end.
I was angry with my foe:
I told it not, my wrath did grow.

And I water'd it in fears, 5
Night and morning with my tears;
And I sunnèd it with smiles
And with soft deceitful wiles.

And it grew both day and night,
Till it bore an apple bright; 10
And my foe beheld it shine,
And he knew that it was mine,

And into my garden stole,
When the night had veil'd the pole:
In the morning glad I see 15
My foe outstretch'd beneath the tree.

WILLIAM BLAKE
(1757–1827)

8 *wiles* – tricks
14 *veil'd the pole* – stretched from the North Pole

Activities

Discussion and notemaking

On your own, study the poem and use the following questions to write down notes of your response. Then, share your ideas in a group or class discussion.

1. In lines 1–2 how does the person deal with their anger and what is the result?
2. In what different situation does the person's anger grow (lines 3–4)?
3. What metaphors in verse 2 reveal that the person's anger continues to grow? What does the person actually do?
4. There are further metaphors in lines 9–14. What do you think is represented by 'an apple bright'? What does 'my garden' represent, and why does his foe enter it stealthily? Discuss how these lines echo the biblical story of the Garden of Eden and what this suggests.
5. What happens in lines 15–16, and how does the person react to it? What moral can be drawn from this outcome?
6. Why is the poem called 'A Poison Tree'? How suitable a title is it?

Speaking and listening

❧ 'It is better to express your anger rather than to repress it.' Discuss this statement in a class debate about anger. Before you begin, look back at your notes on the poem and, in the debate, refer to the ideas that Blake expresses in the poem and say whether or not you agree with them.

Writing

❧ This poem can be read as a **fable** about human behaviour. Explain what its moral is, and write about the imagery Blake uses in order to convey his message.

General Questions

Before you begin answering a question, read each of the poems you are considering writing about. Look at the notes you made when you studied the poem previously, and then read the poem again. Then check that you

- understand what the poem means;
- can say something about your response to a) its tone, b) its language, c) its imagery, and d) its verse form;
- have made up your mind about how the poem affects you;
- are ready to support or argue with the poem's theme.

If necessary, use the Glossary to check the meaning of any technical terms that you want to use when writing about the poem.

1. Dryden and Pope portray public figures in order to make them examples. What do you learn about the poets' reasons for choosing Thomas Shadwell and George Villiers as their victims? Comment on how their weaknesses are described, and the differences you notice between the tone, language and effect of the portraits.
2. Compare the characters of Ulysses and Satan. What qualities do they have in common and what are the main differences between them? Comment on how their characters are revealed by what they have to say and how they say it.
3. Compare the settings and atmospheres which Scott and Wordsworth create in their poems 'Proud Maisie' and 'The Solitary Reaper' and discuss your feelings towards both women.
4. Some poets have strong views about what is wrong with society. What wrongs are dealt with in 'The Slave Mother' and 'The Song of the Shirt'? Which poem in your view more effectively arouses indignation in the reader at those wrongs, and how does it succeed?
5. In which of the poems do you think the poet presents the most detailed portrait of a person? Write about what you learn from the poem about the person, and explain how the poet conveys the main features of their character.
6. Which poem made you feel most strongly about its subject? Discuss why the poem made such an impression on you, and comment on such features as the poet's use of language and imagery, and the form and structure of the poem.
7. Show how the language given to people in *two* of these poems helps to create an impression of what they are really like (for example, in 'The Last Duchess', 'Ulysses', 'The Song of the Shirt').
8. Is satire an effective way of revealing a person's underlying character, or is it a cruel and offensive weapon? Give reasons for your views, and refer to the satirical portraits you have read.

Time and Place

from The Rime of the Ancient Mariner

About the poet

Coleridge (1772–1834) was the youngest of ten children. He went to school in London, then to Cambridge University. While at university he got into debt and joined the army under the name of Silas Tomkyn Comberbache. His family bought him out of the army and he returned to Cambridge but never took a degree. He became friendly with Wordsworth (see page 101) and in 1798 they published a joint volume of poetry entitled *Lyrical Ballads*, which earned them 30 guineas. For much of his adult life Coleridge was addicted to opium, which he started to take in order to relieve pain.

About the poem

Coleridge, with Wordsworth and his sister Dorothy, began a walking holiday along the north coast of Somerset and Devon on 13 November 1797. The poem was half written by the end of the month and finished on 23 March 1798. Coleridge wrote that his aim was to depict 'persons and characters supernatural, or at least romantic ... with this view I wrote my "Ancient Mariner"'. It was the first poem in *Lyrical Ballads*. Coleridge added the marginal comments 20 years later.

The poem, which is a literary ballad, is in seven parts. In Part 1, the mariner tells of his and his shipmates' adventures and sufferings as their ship is driven by storms to the South Pole. Surrounded by ice and fog, they are visited by an albatross, which the mariner impulsively shoots with his crossbow. The following verses are taken from Part 2, in which the ship sails north; the story is told by the mariner.

from The Rime of the Ancient Mariner

The fair breeze blew, the white foam flew,
The furrow followed free;
We were the first that ever burst
Into that silent sea.

The fair breeze continues; the ship enters the Pacific Ocean, and sails northward, even till it reaches the Line.

Down dropt the breeze, the sails dropt down, 5
'Twas sad as sad could be;
And we did speak only to break
The silence of the sea!

The ship hath been suddenly becalmed.

All in a hot and copper sky,
The bloody Sun, at noon, 10
Right up above the mast did stand,
No bigger than the Moon.

Day after day, day after day,
We stuck, nor breath nor motion;
As idle as a painted ship 15
Upon a painted ocean.

Water, water, every where,
And all the boards did shrink;
Water, water, every where,
Nor any drop to drink. 20

And the Albatross begins to be avenged.

The very deep did rot: O Christ!
That ever this should be!
Yea, slimy things did crawl with legs
Upon the slimy sea.

About, about, in reel and rout 25
The death-fires danced at night;
The water, like a witch's oils,
Burnt green, and blue and white.

And some in dreams assurèd were
Of the Spirit that plagued us so; 30
Nine fathom deep he had followed us
From the land of mist and snow.

A Spirit had followed them; one of the invisible inhabitants of this planet, neither departed souls nor angels.

And every tongue, through utter drought,
Was withered at the root;
We could not speak, no more than if 35
We had been choked with soot.

Ah! well a-day! what evil looks
Had I from old and young!
Instead of the cross, the Albatross
About my neck was hung. 40

The shipmates, in their sore distress, would fain throw the whole guilt on the ancient Mariner: in sign whereof they hang the dead sea-bird round his neck.

SAMUEL TAYLOR COLERIDGE
(1772–1834)

15 *painted* – as in a painting
25 *rout* – riot
37 *well a-day!* – alas!

Activities

Discussion and notemaking

Read the poem and in pairs make notes in answer to these questions. Then share your ideas in a class discussion and try to agree an interpretation of the poem.

1. Discuss how Coleridge describes the ship's speedy progress and its sudden becalming in verses 1 and 2. How did its crew feel when the ship was becalmed (lines 7 and 8)?
2. How is the suffering of the crew conveyed in verses 3–5? Discuss the simile used in lines 15–16. What is the effect of the repetition and alliteration in verse 5?
3. What are the mariner's feelings about their situation (verse 6)? What do you think the 'slimy things' are?
4. What do the mariner's shipmates see, imagine and dream (verses 7–8)? What does this tell you about their physical and mental states?
5. Discuss the metaphor in lines 35–36. How does verse 9 convey the crew's great suffering? Mark the stressed syllables in this verse, and discuss how the rhythm of the lines increases their impact.
6. What do the rest of the crew do to the mariner (verse 10)? Discuss why they do it and how the mariner feels.

Speaking and listening

❧ In groups, hotseat the mariner. In pairs draft questions to ask him. Then, during the hotseating, tape-record the mariner's replies, so that you can discuss them afterwards.

Research and writing

❧ Find a copy of the whole poem and read the mariner's description of the South Pole (Part 1 verses 11–15). Does Coleridge create a feeling of cold in those verses as effectively as he creates a feeling of heat in the extract from Part 2?

❧ A contemporary of Coleridge called 'The Ancient Mariner' 'a tale of wonder and mystery'. From what you have read, would you agree with him? Give reasons for your view.

To Autumn

About the poet

John Keats (1795–1821) trained as a medical student. One of his fellow students described him as an idle, loafing fellow, always writing poetry. He quickly established a reputation as one of the leading poets of the time, but died in Rome of tuberculosis when he was only 25.

About the poem

The poem was written in Winchester on 19 September 1819. In a letter to a friend two days later, Keats wrote: 'How beautiful the season is now – I never lik'd stubble fields so much as now – Aye better than the chilly green of the spring. Somehow a stubble plain looks warm – in the same way that some pictures look warm – this struck me so much in my Sunday's walk that I composed upon it.' As well as drawing on his observations of the countryside, Keats was also influenced by landscape paintings such as Poussin's 'Autumn'.

Before reading the poem remind yourself what personification is (see page 28).

To Autumn

I

Season of mists and mellow fruitfulness,
   Close bosom-friend of the maturing sun;
Conspiring with him how to load and bless
   With fruit the vines that round the thatch-eves run;
To bend with apples the moss'd cottage-trees, 5
   And fill all fruit with ripeness to the core;
      To swell the gourd, and plump the hazel shells
   With a sweet kernel; to set budding more,
And still more, later flowers for the bees,
Until they think warm days will never cease, 10
   For summer has o'er-brimm'd their clammy cells.

II

Who hath not seen thee oft amid thy store?
   Sometimes whoever seeks abroad may find
Thee sitting careless on a granary floor,
   Thy hair soft-lifted by the winnowing wind; 15
Or on a half-reap'd furrow sound asleep,
   Drows'd with the fume of poppies, while thy hook
      Spares the next swath and all its twinèd flowers:
And sometimes like a gleaner thou dost keep
   Steady thy laden head across a brook; 20
   Or by a cyder-press, with patient look,
      Thou watchest the last oozings hours by hours.

III

Where are the songs of spring? Ay, where are they?
  Think not of them, thou hast thy music too, –
While barred clouds bloom the soft-dying day, 25
  And touch the stubble-plains with rosy hue;
Then in a wailful choir the small gnats mourn
  Among the river sallows, borne aloft
    Or sinking as the light wind lives or dies;
And full-grown lambs loud bleat from hilly bourn; 30
  Hedge-crickets sing; and now with treble soft
  The red-breast whistles from a garden-croft;
    And gathering swallows twitter in the skies.

John Keats
(1795–1821)

1 *mellow* – soft and rich
3 *conspiring* – working together
7 *gourd* – fruit (e.g. melon)
11 *clammy cells* – sticky honey-combs
14 *careless* – carefree
14 *granary* – store for grain
15 *winnowing* – separating chaff from grain
17 *fume* – sleep-making scent
17 *hook* – reaping-hook
18 *swath* – row of corn
28 *sallows* – willow-trees
30 *bourn* – pasture
32 *garden-croft* – enclosed garden

Activities

Discussion and notemaking

In pairs, make notes to answer these questions, then share your ideas in a group or class discussion.

1. List the features of the autumn scene that are described in verse 1. What impression of autumn does this verse create?
2. Discuss how Keats personifies autumn in verse 2. What human activities does he describe, and what do they suggest about autumn?
3. What sounds are described in verse 3, and what impression of autumn do they give? What does this verse tell you about the poet's attitude to autumn (lines 23, 33)?
4. Discuss those **verbs** in verses 1 and 3 which help Keats to create his portrait of autumn.
5. Re-read both the poem and what Keats said in his letter about autumn. Which of the words from this list best describe how Keats feels about autumn? Can you suggest any others?
   - sad
   - excited
   - thoughtful
   - sentimental
   - animated
   - regretful
   - delighted
   - wistful

Speaking and listening

❧ In groups discuss, your thoughts and feelings about autumn – its sights, sounds and typical activities. Talk about the view of autumn that Keats gives in his poem, and how it compares to your views.

❧ In pairs, imagine you are selecting slides, music and sound effects to accompany a reading of the poem. Discuss the visual images you would choose for each verse, and any music or sound effects that you would include. Make notes of your ideas, then compare them in a class discussion.

Song

About the poet

For details of Percy Bysshe Shelley see page 118.

About the poem

This song is from a verse play *Charles the First*, left unfinished at Shelley's death. It is sung at the end by the Court Fool.

Song

A widow bird sate mourning for her love
  Upon a wintry bough;
The frozen wind crept on above,
  The freezing stream below.

There was no leaf upon the forest bare,   5
  No flower upon the ground,
And little motion in the air
  Except the mill-wheel's sound.

PERCY BYSSHE SHELLEY
(1792–1822)

1 *sate* – sat

Activities

Discussion and notemaking

Study the poem on your own, make notes in answer to the questions, then share your ideas in pairs or groups.

1. What picture is created in the poem? List the details of the winter scene it describes.
2. Pick out the words and phrases which suggest a) it is very cold b) it is still and quiet.
3. Discuss the contrast in lines 7 and 8. How do all the details of the scene combine to create an impression of the bird's grief?
4. Choose one or two adjectives which you think sum up the mood of the poem.

Writing

❧ Write a lyric like Shelley's which describes a scene in order to capture the mood of one of the other seasons. Try to use four-line verses with the rhyme scheme either abab or abcb, and a regular rhythm suitable to the mood you want to create.

A Dirge

About the poet

For details of Percy Bysshe Shelley see page 118.

About the poem

This poem was published after Shelley's death in a collection of *Posthumous Poems*. A dirge is a chant of lamentation for the dead. Before reading the poem remind yourself what alliteration is (see page 18) and what a metaphor is (see page 7).

A Dirge

Rough wind, that moanest loud
   Grief too sad for song;
Wild wind, when sullen cloud
   Knells all the night long;
Sad storm, whose tears are vain, 5
Bare woods, whose branches strain,
Deep caves and dreary main, –
   Wail, for the world's wrong!

PERCY BYSSHE SHELLEY
(1792–1822)

4 *knells* – covers ominously
7 *main* – ocean

Activities

Discussion and notemaking

Study the poem in pairs, making notes in answer to these questions, then share your ideas in a group discussion.

1. What sounds are mentioned in the poem? List the words in the poem that describe them.
2. Discuss the metaphors Shelley uses in lines 1–5. What mood do they help to create?
3. Discuss the effect Shelley's continual use of alliteration has. How does it help create the mood of the poem?
4. What is 'the world's wrong' (line 8)? Which of these phrases best expresses the poet's feeling about the sounds he hears?
   - that nature is making a cry of protest
   - a cry of despair
   - a cry of bewilderment
   - a cry of pity
   - a cry of anguish
   - a cry of grief

Speaking and listening

❧ In groups, rehearse a reading of the poem. Use a synthesiser or some percussion instruments to produce sound effects to accompany your reading and to help you to convey the mood of the poem. Then, perform your reading to the rest of the class, and discuss whose reading is the most effective and why.

Writing

❧ Write a poem in which you use the sights or sounds of nature to express a personal feeling. Choose a verse form similar to Shelley's, in which you can use rhythm and rhyme to help to convey your emotions.

On Wenlock Edge

About the poet

For details of A. E. Housman see page 59.

About the poem

This poem is a lyric – a poem in which the poet's main purpose is to express personal thoughts and feelings. The poem takes the form of a dramatic monologue (see page 95) in which the speaker, an English yeoman, reflects that just as the natural world has always been plagued by storms so humans have always had their troubles.

Housman did not give the poem a title, and it appeared as poem number XXXI in his book *A Shropshire Lad*. Although Housman used real place-names in his poems, the Shropshire about which he wrote was largely an imaginary land. 'I am Worcestershire by birth', Housman wrote in a letter. 'Shropshire was our western horizon, which made me feel romantic about it. I do not know the country well, except in parts, and some of my topographical details are wrong and imaginary.'

Before reading the poem remind yourself what a simile is (see page 26) and what a metaphor is (see page 7).

On Wenlock Edge

On Wenlock Edge the wood's in trouble;
  His forest fleece the Wrekin heaves;
The gale, it plies the saplings double,
  And thick on Severn snow the leaves.

'Twould blow like this through holt and hanger 5
  When Uricon the city stood:
'Tis the old wind in the old anger,
  But then it threshed another wood.

Then, 'twas before my time, the Roman
  At yonder heaving hill would stare: 10
The blood that warms an English yeoman,
  The thoughts that hurt him, they were there.

There, like the wind through woods in riot,
  Through him the gale of life blew high;
The tree of man was never quiet: 15
  Then 'twas the Roman, now 'tis I.

The gale, it plies the saplings double,
  It blows so hard, 'twill soon be gone:
To-day the Roman and his trouble
  Are ashes under Uricon. 20

A. E. HOUSMAN
(1859–1936)

1 *Wenlock Edge* – hill south of Shrewsbury
2 *Wrekin* – hill east of Shrewsbury
5 *holt and hanger* – copse and hill-side wood
6 *Uricon* – Roman name for Wroxeter
11 *yeoman* – historically, owner of small area of land

Activities

Discussion and notemaking

Discuss these questions in pairs, make notes, then share your ideas in either a group or class discussion.

1. List the words and phrases in verse 1 which describe the strength of the gale.
2. What does the yeoman say in verse 2 about the gale and the wood through which it blew in Roman times?
3. In verse 3 how does the yeoman suggest that the sight of the storm-tossed wood has the same effect on both the Roman and him?
4. Discuss the simile in line 13 and the metaphors in lines 14 and 15. How does Housman use the images of the wind and the trees in verse 4 to express the idea that humans have always had their troubles?
5. Discuss the last verse. What does the yeoman say in lines 17 and 18 about the gale? What does he say about the Roman in lines 19 and 20? What do these four lines suggest about how nature's troubles and man's troubles are ended?

Speaking and listening

❧ In groups, discuss the yeoman and decide what his mood is as he speaks this poem. Draft notes for an actor who is going to read the poem, then take it in turns to be the actor and present your reading to the rest of the group. Discuss whose reading worked best and why.

Writing

❧ Trace the development of the yeoman's thoughts throughout the poem. What is his attitude to human misfortune?

The Poplar-Field

About the poet

William Cowper (1731–1800) trained as a lawyer, but a severe mental illness prevented him from taking up a lucrative post as Clerk of the Journals in the House of Lords. He spent a year in an asylum and suffered from recurrences of mental illness throughout his life. He was fortunate enough to have a small private income, and was able, therefore, to develop his interest in writing. He wrote many hymns, and is renowned for his letters as well as his poems.

About the poem

Cowper was fond of walking, and his favourite walk was across a secluded field to the banks of the River Ouse where he could rest from the sun's heat under the shade of a group of poplars. One day in 1784, he arrived to find that the trees had been cut down, and wrote this poem.

Cowper uses a traditional verse form, each stanza consisting of two rhyming couplets. Each line has four stressed syllables and between six and eight unstressed syllables. This variety in line length allows Cowper to vary the poem's pace and mood.

The Poplar-Field

The poplars are fell'd, farewell to the shade
And the whispering sound of the cool colonnade,
The winds play no longer, and sing in the leaves,
Nor Ouse on his bosom their image receives.

Twelve years have elaps'd since I first took a view 5
Of my favourite field and the bank where they grew,
And now in the grass behold they are laid,
And the tree is my seat that once lent me a shade.

The blackbird has fled to another retreat
Where the hazels afford him a screen from the heat, 10
And the scene where his melody charm'd me before,
Resounds with his sweet-flowing ditty no more.

My fugitive years are all hasting away,
And I must ere long lie as lowly as they,
With a turf on my breast, and a stone at my head, 15
Ere another such grove shall arise in its stead.

'Tis a sight to engage me, if any thing can,
To muse on the perishing pleasures of man;
Though his life be a dream, his enjoyments, I see,
Have a being less durable even than he. 20

William Cowper
(1731–1800)

2 *colonnade* – row (of trees, here)
8 *lent me a shade* – gave me a cool shelter
9 *retreat* – place to shelter
10 *afford* – provide
12 *ditty* – song
13 *fugitive* – fleeting
14 *ere* – before
17 *engage* – absorb
18 *muse* – (1) reflect on (2) write a poem about
18 *perishing* – lessening
20 *durable* – lasting

Activities

Discussion and notemaking

In pairs, discuss these questions, make notes of your answers, then share your ideas in a group discussion.

1. Study the first three verses. What do you learn from them about the poet's 'favourite field'? List the various features of the scene that he says have disappeared because the poplars have been felled.
2. Discuss the fourth verse. What thoughts does he express in this verse as a result of comparing his own life to that of the poplars?
3. In the fifth verse, what conclusion does he draw from his reflections?
4. Discuss the following statements. Which of them do you think most accurately summarises what the poem is about?
   - The poet expresses his anger at the destruction of a beautiful scene.
   - The felling of the poplars in his favourite field leads the poet to reflect on his own mortality.
   - The poet thinks about how sad he feels about losing something that has given him so much pleasure.
   - The experience of the poplars being cut down causes the poet to reflect that all good things must come to an end sometime.
   - Some time after he first saw the poplars, their destruction causes the poet immeasurable grief.

Speaking and listening

❧ It has been suggested that the metre of the lines does not suit the feelings that the poet is expressing. In groups, discuss the mood of the poem and how you will need to speak it to make a reading effective. Then, take it in turns to try reading the poem aloud to convey that mood. Present some of your readings to the whole class, and discuss how effective you think the verse form is.

Binsey Poplars

About the poet

Gerard Manley Hopkins (1844–89) was educated at Highgate School and Oxford University. As a young man he became a Roman Catholic, was ordained, and worked as a parish priest before becoming Professor of Greek at the University of Dublin. Hopkins was a friend of Robert Bridges (see page 45). His poetry is characterised by the originality of its language, Hopkins sometimes **coining** new words, creating compound adjectives (for example, by joining words with hyphens), or choosing archaic or dialect words.

About the poem

As a student at Oxford University, Hopkins had often walked along the banks of the River Thames towards the village of Binsey. Taking the same walk 12 years later, he found to his dismay that a great number of aspens which used to line the river had been cut down. The discovery prompted him to write this poem the same day.

Hopkins wrote: 'My poetry is less to be read than to be heard.' In many of his poems, including this one, Hopkins uses an original form of rhythm, which he called **'sprung rhythm'**, a system of stresses and slurs which he developed from his musical background and his reading of Old and Middle English alliterative verse. The poem is printed with marks to indicate these.

Binsey Poplars
felled 1879

'My aspens dear, whose airy cages quelled,
Quelled or quenched in leaves the leaping sun,
All felled, felled, are all felled;
Of a fresh and following folded rank
Not spared, not one 5
That dandled a sandalled
Shadow that swam or sank
On meadow and river and wind-wandering weed-winding bank.'

'O if we but knew what we do
When we delve or hew – 10
Hack and rack the growing green!
Since country is so tender
To touch, her being so slender,
That, like this sleek and seeing ball
But a prick will make no eye at all, 15
Where we, even where we mean
To mend her we end her,
When we hew or delve:
After-comers cannot guess the beauty been.
Ten or twelve, only ten or twelve 20
Strokes of havoc unselve
The sweet especial scene,
Rural scene, a rural scene,
Sweet especial rural scene.'

GERARD MANLEY HOPKINS
(1844–89)

1 *aspens* – poplar trees
1 *quelled* – reduced the heat
2 *quenched* – smothered
6 *dandled* – moved up and down
6 *sandalled* – criss-cross effects of shadows
10 *delve or hew* – dig or cut down
11 *rack* – destroy
13 *slender* – vulnerable
21 *unselve* – destroy the identity of

Activities

Discussion and notemaking

On your own, read the poem through at least twice, then make notes of a) words or phrases that you find striking or effective b) phrases or lines which particularly reveal the poet's thinking and feeling. Then share your ideas in groups and discuss the following questions, making notes of your answers.

1. What details of the riverside scene are described at the beginning and end of verse 1 (lines 1–2, 6–8)? Discuss the metaphors used to describe the sunlight shining through the trees and on the river. What impression do they create of the scene?
2. What is the effect of the use of repetition in line 3, and how does line 5 add to that effect?
3. Which lines in verse 2 suggest that man is unthinkingly destroying nature?
4. Discuss the comparison in lines 14 and 15. What does it suggest about how vulnerable nature is? Which other words or phrases in verse 2 suggest how fragile nature is?
5. Which words and phrases in verse 2 suggest that man's destruction of nature is violent?
6. How does the poet feel about the felling of the poplars? Which lines in the poem most clearly convey to you his emotions?

Speaking and listening

❧ Imagine that instead of expressing his thoughts about the felling of the poplars in a poem, the person in the poem telephoned a friend. In pairs, role play the conversation in which he expresses his feelings about the poplars being cut down.

❧ In pairs or groups, discuss what effect you would want a reading of the poem to have on its audience. Then plan and rehearse speaking the poem to fit the stresses marked. Perform some of your readings to the rest of the class, and discuss which were the most effective and why.

Writing

❧ Re-read the poem, looking carefully at its language. In one column, write down two examples of each of the following, and in the adjoining one their effects.

- unusual word order
- repetition
- alliteration
- compressed phrases
- words that Hopkins made up (coinages)

Then use your notes to help you to draft an essay answering this question:

'What thoughts and feelings about the felling of the trees does Hopkins express in his poem "Binsey Poplars"? Comment on the effects of the way Hopkins uses language in the poem to convey what he thinks and feels.'

Slow Spring

About the poet

The daughter of an Irish farmer, Katharine Tynan (1861–1931) began writing at the age of 17. She was a friend of W. B. Yeats (see page 74), and played a leading part in the movement to encourage Irish culture and writing about Irish life. She was a prolific author, writing more than a hundred novels and several volumes of autobiography.

About the poem

This is a short lyric poem in which the poet expresses her feelings about the developing spring. The poem consists of two four-line verses in which lines 2 and 4 rhyme and in which there are internal rhymes in lines 1 and 3.

Slow Spring

O year, grow slowly. Exquisite, holy,
  The days go on
With almonds showing the pink stars blowing,
  And birds in the dawn.

Grow slowly, year, like a child that is dear, 5
  Or a lamb that is mild,
By little steps, and by little skips,
  Like a lamb or a child.

KATHARINE TYNAN
(1861–1931)

1 *exquisite* – extremely beautiful
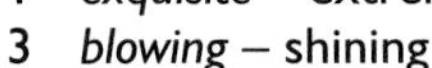
3 *blowing* – shining

Activities

Discussion and notemaking

Study the poem on your own. Make notes in answer to these questions, then share your ideas in a group discussion.

1. What do you learn from the first line about the poet's feelings about spring? Why does she want the year to 'grow slowly'?
2. What two features of spring are described in lines 3 and 4? What impression of spring do these two images create?
3. In the second verse, what two comparisons does the poet use? What do they suggest about the spring? What do they tell you about her feelings?

Speaking and listening

In pairs, make notes about how the poem should be read aloud. Notice how the poem consists mainly of one-syllable words, and how this helps to slow down the pace and to suggest the slow development of spring that the poet yearns for. Take it in turns to read the poem aloud. Perform some of your readings to the rest of the class, and discuss which readings most successfully convey the feelings the poet expresses in the poem.

Home-Thoughts from Abroad

About the poet

For details of Robert Browning see page 35.

About the poem

This poem was published in November 1845 and was almost certainly written during a visit to Italy the previous year.

It is written in two stanzas of different lengths which are irregularly rhymed.

Home-Thoughts from Abroad

Oh, to be in England
Now that April's there,
And whoever wakes in England
Sees, some morning, unaware,
That the lowest boughs and the brushwood sheaf 5
Round the elm-tree bole are in tiny leaf,
While the chaffinch sings on the orchard bough
In England – now!

And after April, when May follows,
And the whitethroat builds, and all the swallows! 10
Hark, where my blossomed pear-tree in the hedge
Leans to the field and scatters on the clover
Blossoms and dewdrops – at the bent spray's edge –
That's the wise thrush; he sings each song twice over,
Lest you should think he never could recapture 15
The first fine careless rapture!
And though the fields look rough with hoary dew,
All will be gay when noontide wakes anew
The buttercups, the little children's dower
– Far brighter than this gaudy melon-flower! 20

ROBERT BROWNING
(1812–89)

6 *bole* – trunk
10 *whitethroat* – warbler
17 *hoary* – white-looking
19 *dower* – nature's gift

Activities

Discussion and notemaking

Discuss these questions in groups. Make notes of your answers, then share your ideas in a class discussion.

1. Discuss the first stanza. Why does the person in the poem wish that they were in England in April? What two features of the natural world does the poet use as typical of April in England? What do they suggest happens in England in April?
2. List the sights and sounds that the poet remembers in lines 9–16 about England during May. What do these lines tell you about his feelings?
3. Discuss lines 17–20. What contrasts does the poet use to suggest how beautiful England seems compared to Italy?
4. How would you describe the mood of this poem? Which word(s) from the list below do you think most accurately describe the poem's mood? Can you suggest any others?
   - melancholic
   - regretful
   - wistful
   - cheerful
   - delightful
   - yearning
   - nostalgic

Speaking and listening

❧ In pairs, role play a conversation about England between two people who are living abroad in springtime. One of them expresses a similar view to the person in the poem, the other takes a different view and says that they are glad to be abroad.

Writing

❧ Use the ideas expressed in the poem and write the letter or the postcard that the person might have written to a friend at home, if they had chosen to convey their thoughts in prose rather than poetry.

❧ Write your own poem expressing your thoughts and feelings about England in springtime. Choose a verse form which suits the ideas you wish to convey.

Spring Quiet

About the poet

For details of Christina Rossetti see page 7.

About the poem

This poem was written in 1847, when Christina Rossetti was a teenager. In it a person looks forward to the coming of spring and imagines the comfort it will bring her. The poem is written in four-line verses with the rhyme scheme abcb.

Spring Quiet

Gone were but the Winter,
   Come were but the Spring,
I would go to a covert
   Where the birds sing;

Where in the whitethorn (5)
   Singeth a thrush,
And a robin sings
   In the holly-bush.

Full of fresh scents
   Are the budding boughs (10)
Arching high over
   A cool green house:

Full of sweet scents,
And whispering air
Which sayeth softly: 15
'We spread no snare;

'Here dwell in safety,
Here dwell alone,
With a clear stream
And a mossy stone. 20

'Here the sun shineth
Most shadily;
Here is heard an echo
Of the far sea,
Tho' far off it be.' 25

CHRISTINA ROSSETI
(1830–94)

3 *covert* – shelter, thicket

Activities

Discussion and notemaking

In pairs, discuss these questions, make notes of your answers, then share your ideas in a group or a class discussion.

1. What kind of place does the person imagine going to when spring comes? What do the sounds and smells described in verses 2, 3 and 4 suggest about the place?
2. Which words and phrases in verses 4, 5 and 6 suggest that the place she imagines is peaceful and safe?
3. Notice how, by putting an extra line in the final verse, the poet draws attention to the phrase 'Tho' far off it be'. What does this suggest about the coming of spring and the place she is imagining?
4. Do you think 'Spring Quiet' is a suitable title? Does it sum up the mood of the poem? Suggest some alternative titles.

Speaking and listening

❧ In groups, discuss the personification of the place in verses 4–6 and the effect this has. Then, rehearse a reading of the poem. Before you begin, discuss the impression you want your reading to have on those listening to it, and experiment with different combinations of voices in order to achieve that effect. Perform your reading for the rest of the class, and discuss which reading is the most effective and why.

Dover Beach

About the poet

Matthew Arnold (1822–88) was the son of Thomas Arnold, the famous headmaster of Rugby public school. Matthew Arnold was a scholar who was very interested in education, and for over 30 years he was an inspector of schools. In addition to poetry, he wrote books on literary criticism, religion and education. In 1857 he became the first Professor of Poetry at Oxford University.

About the poem

In this poem Arnold describes his thoughts and feelings looking out to sea from Dover beach. At least part of the poem was written during a visit to Dover which Arnold made with his wife in June 1851, shortly after their marriage. The poem consists of four unequal verse-paragraphs with irregular rhyme schemes.

Dover Beach

The sea is calm to-night.
The tide is full, the moon lies fair
Upon the straits; – on the French coast the light
Gleams and is gone; the cliffs of England stand,
Glimmering and vast, out in the tranquil bay. 5
Come to the window, sweet is the night-air!
Only, from the long line of spray
Where the sea meets the moon-blanch'd land,
Listen! you hear the grating roar
Of pebbles which the waves draw back, and fling, 10
At their return, up the high strand,
Begin, and cease, and then again begin,
With tremulous cadence slow, and bring
The eternal note of sadness in.

Sophocles long ago 15
Heard it on the Aegean, and it brought
Into his mind the turbid ebb and flow
Of human misery; we
Find also in the sound a thought,
Hearing it by this distant northern sea. 20

The Sea of Faith
Was once, too, at the full, and round earth's shore
Lay like the folds of a bright girdle furl'd.
But now I only hear
Its melancholy, long, withdrawing roar, 25
Retreating, to the breath
Of the night-wind, down the vast edges drear
And naked shingles of the world.

Ah, love, let us be true
To one another! for the world, which seems 30
To lie before us like a land of dreams,
So various, so beautiful, so new,
Hath really neither joy, nor love, nor light,
Nor certitude, nor peace, nor help for pain;
And we are here as on a darkling plain 35
Swept with confused alarms of struggle and flight,
Where ignorant armies clash by night.

MATTHEW ARNOLD
(1822–88)

5 *tranquil* – calm
8 *-blanch'd* – -whitened
11 *strand* – beach
13 *tremulous cadence* – uncertain, varying pitch
17 *turbid* – confused
23 *furl'd* – rolled up
34 *certitude* – feeling of certainty
35 *darkling* – dark
36 *alarms* – warnings of danger

Activities

Discussion and notemaking

In groups, discuss these questions, make notes of your ideas, then share them in a class discussion.

1. List the details of the scene that are described in lines 1–6. Discuss Arnold's choice of adjectives. What is the mood of these lines?
2. What sound is described in lines 7–14? How does the poet react to the sound? What does he think and feel about it (lines 12–14)?
3. What thoughts does Arnold suggest he shares with Sophocles (lines 15–20)? Discuss how the second verse-paragraph develops the mood created at the end of the first.
4. Discuss how in the third verse-paragraph Arnold uses the sea and its changing tides as a metaphor to describe the decline of his religious belief. Which words and phrases express Arnold's feelings of loss and dismay?
5. What view of the world does Arnold convey in lines 29–37? What is the contrast Arnold makes in these lines between the world as it seems to be and the world as it really is?
6. Study the image he uses in lines 35–37. Which words and phrases suggest darkness and violence? How do these lines convey the idea that humans are involved in a spiritual conflict that they cannot win?
7. The mood of the final section contrasts with the mood of the first six lines. Discuss how the mood changes and develops in the poem.

Speaking and listening

❧ In groups, imagine you are producing a radio series called 'Poems in Perspective' and have decided to focus on 'Dover Beach' in a forthcoming programme. You plan to include an item consisting of an introduction to the poem, a reading of it, and a follow-up discussion of its language and meaning. Together, draft an introduction and make notes for the actor who is going to read the poem, offering advice on how to read it to show the changes in mood and to convey the different thoughts that are expressed in the four sections. Make a list of the key points that you want to make in the follow-up discussion. Then, rehearse the whole item, tape-record it, and play your tape-recordings to the rest of the class.

Writing

❧ Write the entry in a journal that the poet might have written if he had decided to express his thoughts and feelings in prose rather than poetry.

❧ Trace the development of Arnold's thoughts and feelings in this poem, and explain how he uses descriptions and images of the sea to convey his beliefs.

It was night and on the mountains

About the poet

For details of Emily Brontë see page 26.

About the poem

Although the poem was written in 1843, it remained undiscovered among the poet's manuscripts until it was published in 1902. The poem is written in four-line stanzas with the rhyme scheme abab. The a rhymes are **feminine rhymes** and the metre is **trochaic**. In describing an event in the past, the poet suggests the peasant's sense of loss, and the choice of metre helps to do this.

It was night and on the mountains

It was night and on the mountains
Fathoms deep the snow drifts lay
Streams and waterfalls and fountains
Down in darkness stole away

Long ago the hopeless peasant 5
Left his sheep all buried there
Sheep that through the summer pleasant
He had watched with fondest care

Now no more a cheerful ranger
Following pathways known of yore 10
Sad he stood a wildered stranger
On his own unbounded moor

EMILY JANE BRONTË
(1818–48)

4 *stole* – flowed silently
9 *ranger* – wanderer
10 *of yore* – in earlier times
11 *wildered* – bewildered, confused

Activities

Discussion and notemaking

In pairs, discuss these questions, make notes of your answers, then share your ideas in a group discussion.

1. What details of the scene are described in the first verse? What impression do they give you of the scene? What does the phrase 'stole away' (line 4) suggest?
2. Study verse 2. What do you learn about the shepherd and his sheep from lines 5–6? What do lines 7 and 8 tell you about them? Discuss how these lines provide a contrast with lines 5 and 6.
3. Discuss verse 3. Pick out the words and phrases which tell you what the shepherd is feeling. How and why have his feelings changed?
4. How would you describe the mood of the poem? Choose two or three words which you think sum up this mood.
5. This poem was not given a title by the author, so editors often use the first line as its title. Suggest an alternative title for the poem.

Speaking and listening

❧ Imagine you have been commissioned to design a series of poetry posters and that this poem is to be featured on one of them. Discuss your ideas for the poster with a partner, and then take it in turns to present them to the rest of the group.

❧ The manuscript version of the poem includes the following lines, between verses 1 and 2, which were crossed out by the poet:

> Cold and wild the wind was blowing
> Keen and clear the heaven above
> But though countless stars were glowing
> Absent was the star of love.

In groups, read the poem with this extra verse included. First, you will need to punctuate the verse. Discuss whether it adds anything to the poem and suggest why the poet decided to delete it.

Writing

❧ You are preparing a poetry anthology which is to include Emily Brontë's poem and have to decide whether or not to include the extra verse. Write a letter to the publisher explaining your decision.

Inversnaid

About the poet

For details of Gerard Manley Hopkins see page 138.

About the poem

Hopkins had begun to draft the poem that became 'Inversnaid' in February 1879, writing in a letter: 'I have something if only I could seize it on the decline of wild nature, beginning somehow like this:

O where is it, the wildness,
The wildness of the wilderness?'

What prompted him to recall the idea and finish the poem was a visit he made to Loch Lomond and Inversnaid two and a half years later, in September 1881, where he observed a stream tumbling into the loch. The scene that inspired him has been described as follows: 'Arklet Water was wider and fuller than a burn; its peaty-brown waters, descended from Loch Arklet, were added to by burns, noticeably Snaid Burn, and over a course of a mile and a half through narrow valleys of heather and ladder-fern to oak forests, with the occasional birch, ash, and, hanging over the water, rowan, gradually steepened and quickened. There were smaller falls and side pools, with froth, foam, bubbles, and whirls, in rocky basins, before the final, magnificent, high but broken fall into a larger pool just before it entered Loch Lomond.' (Taken from Norman White, *Hopkins: A Literary Life.*)

Unlike 'Binsey Poplars' (see page 139), the poem has a traditional form. It consists of four verses, each having two rhyming couplets. Most lines have four stresses, though the number of unstressed syllables varies.

Inversnaid

This darksome burn, horseback brown,
His rollrock highroad roaring down,
In coop and in comb the fleece of his foam
Flutes and low to the lake falls home.

A windpuff-bonnet of fáwn-fróth 5
Turns and twindles over the broth
Of a pool so pitchblack, féll-frówning,
It rounds and rounds Despair to drowning.

Degged with dew, dappled with dew
Are the groins of the braes that the brook treads through, 10
Wiry heathpacks, flitches of fern,
And the beadbonny ash that sits over the burn.

What would the world be, once bereft
Of wet and of wildness? Let them be left,
O let them be left, wildness and wet; 15
Long live the weeds and the wilderness yet.

GERARD MANLEY HOPKINS
(1844–89)

3 *coop and comb* – hollow and crest
4 *flutes* – makes grooves
6 *twindles* – a blend of 'twist' and 'dwindle'
9 *Degged* – sprinkled (Lancashire dialect)
dappled – spotted
10 *groins* – lower parts
10 *braes* – hillsides
11 *flitches* – tufts
12 *beadbonny* – attractive bead-like orange berries
13 *bereft* – deprived

Activities

Discussion and notemaking

On your own, study the poem and write down what these phrases and coinages suggest to you.

- 'horseback brown' (line 1)
- 'rollrock highroad' (line 2)
- 'windpuff-bonnet of fawn-froth' (line 5)
- 'twindles' (line 6)
- 'fell-frowning' (line 7)
- 'degged' (line 9)
- 'wiry heathpacks' (line 11)
- 'beadbonny ash' (line 12)

Next, in groups compare your ideas and discuss these questions, making notes of your answers.

1. What impression of the burn is created in verse 1? Discuss the words and phrases which create that impression.
2. What details of the pool are given in verse 2? What are the poet's thoughts and feelings as he contemplates the pool? What is your interpretation of line 8?
3. How do the details of the scene described in verse 3 and the rhythm of the verse provide a contrast with verse 2? How is the poet's mood in verse 3 different from his mood at the end of verse 2?
4. What thoughts and feelings about the scene does the poet express in verse 4? What is the effect of the alliteration and repetition in this verse?

Speaking and listening

❧ In pairs, look back to 'Binsey Poplars' and how it is marked, then read through 'Inversnaid' and mark it for reading aloud. Compare your markings with those of other pairs, and then rehearse reading the poem aloud. Choose some people to perform their readings to the class, and discuss which reading is the most effective.

❧ In groups, make a collage consisting of words and phrases from the poem and pictures from old newspapers and magazines in order to illustrate the thoughts and feelings expressed in 'Inversnaid'. Then take it in turns to show your collages to each other and to explain your choice of pictures.

Writing

❧ Find a photograph or painting of a scene which you find striking for some reason. Try to write a poem conveying your thoughts and feelings about the scene, in the style that Hopkins uses in his poems. Before drafting your poem, write down which features of his style you are going to try to imitate.

❧ What is Hopkins's attitude to nature and what man does to nature? How are his thoughts and feelings about nature conveyed in 'Binsey Poplars' and 'Inversnaid'?

❧ Hopkins wrote: 'No doubt my poetry errs on the side of oddness.' Describe the main differences between his poetry and that of other poets you have read. Refer to 'Binsey Poplars' and 'Inversnaid' and comment on any particular effects that Hopkins achieves through their 'oddness'.

London

About the poet

For details of William Blake see page 121.

About the poem

Blake wrote at a time of revolutionary change in Europe. There was hostility to the monarchy and the Church, which were accused of being the cause of ordinary people's sufferings. He felt that, in London as in other cities and towns, charters which were supposed to protect individual freedom in fact restricted it, because they put civic control in the hands of a few guilds or companies. Blake agreed with Thomas Paine that a charter 'operates by taking rights away'. He was angry that people tolerated such constraints: he wrote, 'Their minds are fetter'd; then how can they be free?'

Blake lived all his life in London, and in this poem chooses details which show how it has changed since he was a boy enjoying 'the fields from Islington to Marybone'.

London

I wander thro' each charter'd street
Near where the charter'd Thames does flow,
And mark in every face I meet
Marks of weakness, marks of woe.

In every cry of every Man, 5
In every Infant's cry of fear,
In every voice, in every ban,
The mind-forg'd manacles I hear:

How the Chimney-sweeper's cry
Every black'ning Church appals, 10
And the hapless Soldier's sigh
Runs in blood down Palace walls.

But most thro' midnight streets I hear
How the youthful Harlot's curse
Blasts the new born Infant's tear, 15
And blights with plagues the Marriage hearse.

William Blake
(1757–1827)

1 *charter'd* – regulated; Blake first wrote 'dirty'
3 *mark* – notice
4 *marks* – signs
7 *ban* – curse
8 *mind-forg'd* – people's freedom is limited by the restrictions they accept
8 *manacles* – handcuffs (metaphor)
9 *Chimney-sweeper's* – children as young as 8 years old were employed as sweeps
14 *curse* – (1) verbal abuse (2) sexually transmitted disease
16 *hearse* – (1) loveless marriage is a living death (2) the disease causes death

Activities

Discussion and notemaking

On your own, read the poem and make notes in two columns of the impression Blake gives of what it is like to live in London now and in the past. Then in groups compare your notes, and revise them by discussing answers to the following questions.

1. How in verses 1 and 2 does Blake build up the impression of people's suffering?
2. Study lines 1–2 and line 8. What do they suggest about what is responsible for causing people's suffering?
3. What does verse 3 suggest about the effect of the Church and the monarchy on people's lives?
4. What feature of London life is described in verse 4? How do the words and phrases Blake uses in lines 15–16 emphasise people's suffering?

Speaking and listening

❧ In pairs, use the resources centre to research what life was like for ordinary people in London in the late eighteenth and early nineteenth centuries. Prepare a short factual talk to present to the class describing what Blake would have seen as he wandered round London.

❧ In pairs, imagine you have been asked to do a series of drawings or to make a series of slides to illustrate the poem. Decide which lines you would illustrate and make notes of your ideas, then share them in a group discussion. You could then make rough sketches of your ideas with the lines written underneath, and put them up as a wall display.

Writing

❧ Write one or two paragraphs, explaining your reactions to the poem and your interpretation of it, designed to help a student of your age to understand it.

❧ What impression of life in London does the poem give? What does Blake reveal of his thoughts and feelings about London?

General Questions

Before you begin answering a question, read each of the poems you are considering writing about. Look at the notes you made when you studied the poem previously, and then read the poem again. Then check that you

- understand what the poem means;
- can say something about your response to a) its tone, b) its language, c) its imagery, and d) its verse form;
- have made up your mind about how the poem affects you;
- are ready to support or argue with the poem's theme.

If necessary, use the Glossary to check the meaning of any technical terms that you want to use when writing about the poem.

1. Compare 'The Poplar-Field' and 'Binsey Poplars', commenting on any similarities and contrasts in the two poems. In your opinion, which poem more effectively conveys the poet's thought and feelings? Give reasons for your view.
2. Compare the language and verse form of 'Spring Quiet' and 'It was night and on the mountain'. Discuss how each suits the theme and mood of its poem. Explain which you find the more effective.
3. Select *two* poems that are about places and write about them comparing the locations that are described and commenting on any similarities and differences between the two poems.
4. Choose *two or three* poems in this section which convey the poet's love of nature. Write about the different ways that the poets express their feelings, commenting in particular on the language and imagery they use to convey their emotions.
5. Discuss the contrast between the theme which Housman writes about in 'On Wenlock Edge' and that of Arnold's 'On Dover Beach'. Explain how the scene described in each poem relates to its theme.
6. In many of the poems in this section, the poets use a description of a time or a place to express their personal emotions. Choose *two or three* poems which express personal emotions. Comment on their language, imagery, style and structure, and say in which one you think the strength of the poet's feelings is most effectively conveyed.
7. It has been suggested that 'Home-Thoughts from Abroad', 'London' and 'On Wenlock Edge' should have been placed in the Reflections section rather than in this section. Argue the case *either* that they belong in this section *or* that they should have come under Reflections.
8. Choose any *three* poems from this section which show how different poems about times and places can be. Comment on the range of subjects that poets choose, the different emotions that they express, and the variety of verse forms, language, imagery and techniques that they use.

Reflections

The Wild Swans at Coole

About the poet

For details of W. B. Yeats see page 74.

About the poem

This poem was written in October 1916 while Yeats was staying at Coole Park, Galway, the home of Sir William and Lady Gregory. Yeats was 51 when he wrote the poem, and he reflects how much he has changed since he first visited Coole almost 20 years earlier. At the time of writing, he was deeply depressed because of an unhappy love affair. At Coole he gradually recovered his health, and during visits over many years worked in a room looking out towards the lake.

The poem is written in six-line stanzas with the rhyme scheme abcbdd.

The Wild Swans at Coole

The trees are in their autumn beauty,
The woodland paths are dry,
Under the October twilight the water
Mirrors a still sky;
Upon the brimming water among the stones 5
Are nine-and-fifty swans.

The nineteenth autumn has come upon me
Since I first made my count;
I saw, before I had well finished,
All suddenly mount 10
And scatter wheeling in great broken rings
Upon their clamorous wings.

I have looked upon those brilliant creatures,
And now my heart is sore.
All's changed since I, hearing at twilight, 15
The first time on this shore,
The bell-beat of their wings above my head,
Trod with a lighter tread.

Unwearied still, lover by lover,
They paddle in the cold 20
Companionable streams or climb the air;
Their hearts have not grown old;
Passion or conquest, wander where they will,
Attend upon them still.

But now they drift on the still water, 25
Mysterious, beautiful;
Among what rushes will they build,
By what lake's edge or pool
Delight men's eyes when I awake some day
To find they have flown away? 30

W. B. YEATS
(1865–1939)

12 *clamorous* – noisy 24 *attend upon* – go with

Activities

Discussion and notemaking

Discuss these questions in pairs, each make notes of your ideas, then share them in a class discussion.

1. List the details of the scene that are described in lines 1–6. What impression of the scene is given in these lines?
2. What happened while the poet was counting the swans (lines 7–12)? How did this alter the scene, and how does it alter the mood of the poem?
3. What do you learn in the third stanza about how the poet's feelings have changed since he first saw the swans? What has made his heart sore?
4. Pick out the words and phrases in stanza 4 which show that the swans have not changed. How does the poet use the description of the swans' unchanging behaviour to provide a contrast with his own feelings?
5. What picture of the swans is given in lines 25–26? What does the **rhetorical question** in lines 27–30 suggest the poet feels about them delighting someone else by another lake or pool?

Speaking and listening

❧ In pairs, role play a scene in which the poet talks to Lady Gregory and discusses his feelings about being at Coole.

Writing

❧ Write a letter to a friend that Yeats might have written from Coole, describing seeing the swans and the thoughts and feelings that he experienced.

from Lines Composed a Few Miles Above Tintern Abbey

About the poet

For details of William Wordsworth see page 101.

About the poem

The full title of the poem is 'Lines written a few miles above Tintern Abbey, on revisiting the banks of the Wye during a tour, July 13, 1798'. Wordsworth had first visited the Wye Valley in 1793, after walking largely without food across Salisbury Plain. His second visit was made in 1798 during a walking tour with his sister Dorothy, in which they covered 20 miles a day. He is reminded how important the landscape near Tintern Abbey has been to him during those five years, and the poem describes what he feels rather than what he sees. He wrote the poem quickly, and it was printed last in *Lyrical Ballads*, which was published later in 1798. His choice of blank verse, with no stanza breaks and no constraints of rhyme, allows the movement of the poem to capture the slow development of his reflective, inquiring thinking.

from Tintern Abbey

Though absent long,
These forms of beauty have not been to me
As is a landscape to a blind man's eye:
But oft, in lonely rooms, and mid the din
Of towns and cities, I have owed to them 5
In hours of weariness sensations sweet
Felt in the blood, and felt along the heart,
And passing even into my purer mind
With tranquil restoration – feelings too
Of unremembered pleasure: such, perhaps, 10
As may have had no trivial influence
On that best portion of a good man's life,
His little nameless unremembered acts
Of kindness and of love. Nor less, I trust,
To them I may have owed another gift, 15
Of aspect more sublime: that blessed mood
In which the burthen of the mystery,
In which the heavy and the weary weight
Of all this unintelligible world,
Is lightened – that serene and blessed mood 20
In which the affections gently lead us on,
Until, the breath of this corporeal frame
And even the motion of our human blood
Almost suspended, we are laid asleep
In body and become a living soul, 25
While, with an eye made quiet by the power
Of harmony and the deep power of joy,
We see into the life of things.

William Wordsworth
(1770–1850)

4 *mid* – amid
9 *tranquil restoration* – restoring a sense of calmness
11 *no trivial* – quite an important
16 *of aspect more sublime* – of more precious quality
17 *burthen* – burden
22 *corporeal frame* – body
24 *suspended* – stopped

Activities

Discussion and notemaking

Study the poem and the background information in the section 'About the poem'. Either on your own or in pairs, make notes which answer these questions. Then in larger groups discuss how to improve your answers.

1. How does the simile in line 3 emphasise how vivid the landscape has remained in Wordsworth's mind?
2. Write down phrases from lines 4–10 which most clearly show the importance of the memories to Wordsworth. What effects did they have on him?
3. In lines 10–14, Wordsworth suggests that his memories have affected his behaviour. In what ways?
4. In lines 14–20, Wordsworth begins to describe the spiritual experience that his memories have created. What does he say about the mood that they formed?
5. List the words and phrases from lines 20–25 which most effectively describe the mood he experienced.
6. In lines 26–28 Wordsworth finally describes the mystical experience which contemplating his memories has produced. In your own words, describe the main features of this experience, and then compare your words with Wordsworth's.

Speaking and listening

❧ In pairs, discuss any parts of the extract that puzzle you, and discuss the questions you would need Wordsworth to answer to help you to understand them.

❧ The extract consists of only two sentences. It is reflective and describes a personal religious experience. In groups, discuss the difficulties these features make for reading the poem aloud, and how you might solve them. Then, on your own, rehearse a reading of the poem. Choose some people to perform their readings to the class, and discuss whose reading was the most successful.

Writing

❧ At the beginning of the extract, Wordsworth is remembering the beauty of the landscape up-stream of Tintern Abbey. At the end, he is claiming insight into the 'life of things'. Trace the stages through which his thinking passes.

❧ A commentator said, 'The poet is the subject of these lines, not Tintern Abbey'. Explain why you agree or disagree with this statement.

There Came a Wind like a Bugle

About the poet

Emily Dickinson (1830–86) was an American poet born in Amherst, Massachusetts, a small and rigid community where the Church held the highest authority. She retreated into her own world constructed from knowledge of the local natural world and of books smuggled into the house by her lawyer brother. She wrote about 1,800 poems, but only 7 were published during her lifetime. She liked being on her own, and during her forties she began to spend more and more time alone in her room. She wore only white and rarely came downstairs. But in her poetry she was witty, rebellious and original.

About the poem

Emily Dickinson describes a summer thunderstorm and uses the symbol of the storm to make a statement about life. Notice the punctuation of the poem: it is unusual because of the way the poet uses capital letters for certain words, and dashes rather than other punctuation marks. The dashes act as punctuation marks, rather than as breaks in the poet's thoughts, and show you when to pause when you are reading the poem aloud.

There Came a Wind like a Bugle

There came a Wind like a Bugle –
It quivered through the Grass
And a Green Chill upon the Heat
So ominous did pass
We barred the Windows and the Doors 5
As from an Emerald Ghost –
The Doom's electric Moccasin
That very instant passed –
On a strange Mob of panting Trees
And Fences fled away 10
And Rivers where the Houses ran
Those looked that lived – that Day –
The Bell within the steeple wild
The flying tidings told –
How much can come 15
And much can go,
And yet abide the World!

EMILY DICKINSON
(1830–86)

4 *ominous* – threatening disaster
7 *Moccasin* – poisonous American snake (metaphor)
14 *told* – (1) announced (2) tolled
17 *abide the world* – the world continues

Activities

Discussion and notemaking Discuss these questions in groups. Each make notes of your ideas, then share them in a class discussion.

1. How does Emily Dickinson suggest in lines 1–4 that a storm is coming? What does the simile in line 1 suggest about the sound and strength of the wind? Which words and phrases in lines 2–4 create an atmosphere of foreboding?
2. How do lines 5 and 6 reinforce the idea that a violent storm is coming? What does the image of 'an Emerald Ghost' suggest? Discuss how this image builds upon and echoes the images used in lines 2 and 3.
3. What do you understand by the phrase 'The Doom's electric Moccasin' (line 7)? Talk about each word in turn and discuss what it suggests to you about the storm.
4. What do lines 9–12 tell you about the devastation caused by the storm? Discuss the metaphors that Emily Dickinson uses to describe the destruction.
5. Discuss Emily Dickinson's use of the symbol of the storm (lines 13–17) to make a statement about life. What are 'the flying tidings' that the storm brings? What effect is created by the fact that it is 'The Bell within the steeple wild' that brings these tidings? What does the use of the word 'told' suggest? Discuss the poet's the use of personification and wordplay in these lines.
6. How would you sum up the mood of this poem? How does the poet's use of colour (lines 1–6) affect the mood of the poem?

Speaking and listening ❧ Work either in pairs or groups. Make a collage, either by drawing your own pictures or finding pictures in old newspapers and magazines, to build up a pictorial illustration of the images Emily Dickinson uses in this poem. Then take it in turns to present your collage to the rest of the class, explaining how your choice of pictures expresses your understanding of the poem.

Writing ❧ Discuss how Emily Dickinson creates a picture of a summer thunderstorm in 'There Came a Wind like a Bugle' and uses the storm as a symbol to make a statement about life. Comment on the language and imagery she uses, and say how effective you think it is. Give reasons for your views.

It is not growing like a tree

About the poet

Ben Jonson (1572–1637) was famous as a playwright and writer of court masques – entertainments which included pantomime, dancing, dialogues and songs. His father died before he was born and, after leaving school, Jonson worked as a bricklayer, soldier and actor, before starting to write plays. In 1598, he was imprisoned for a short time, following a duel in which he killed another actor. His famous plays include the satirical comedies *Volpone* and *The Alchemist.*

About the poem

In this poem, as in his other writing, Jonson expresses his views directly and confidently. He uses images drawn from the natural world to present his view of how to judge goodness in a person. The verse pattern, with lines of different lengths, helps to communicate his quiet certainty. The belief he expresses in the last couplet also occurs in a poem he wrote on the death of his first son on the latter's eighth birthday.

It is not growing like a tree

It is not growing like a tree
In bulk, doth make Man better be;
Or standing long an oak, three hundred year,
To fall a log at last, dry, bald, and sere:
A lily of a day 5
Is fairer far in May,
Although it fall and die that night;
It was the plant and flower of Light.
In small proportions we just beauties see;
And in short measures life may perfect be. 10

Ben Jonson
(1572–1637)

2 *bulk* – size
2 *doth make* – makes
4 *sere* – dried up
5 *of a day* – which lasts one day
10 *short measures* – brief existence

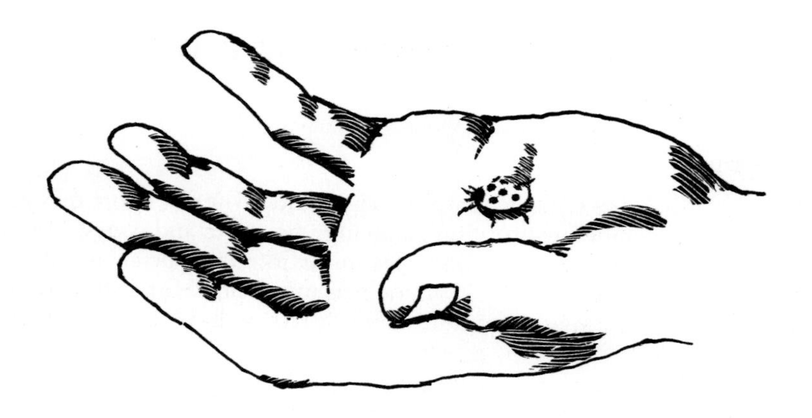

Activities

Discussion and notemaking

In pairs, discuss these questions. Make notes of your answers, then share your ideas in a group discussion.

1. Discuss the comparisons in lines 1–4. What human characteristics do they suggest? What is the poet's attitude towards such characteristics?
2. What features of the lily are described in lines 5–8? Suggest what the lily symbolises, and discuss how the lily provides a contrast with the oak.
3. In your own words, explain the view that Jonson expresses in the last two lines of the poem.
4. Suggest an alternative title for the poem. Try to find one that sums up the view that the poet is expressing.

Speaking and listening

❧ On your own, make a sketch of your ideas for a poster to illustrate the ideas and images in the poem. Then, share your ideas in a group discussion.

Writing

❧ What views does Jonson express in his poem 'It is not growing like a tree'? Explain how the imagery and the verse form help him to convey his views.

Virtue

About the poet

George Herbert (1593–1633) was educated at Westminster School and at Trinity College, Cambridge University. He was a successful scholar, becoming a Fellow of Trinity and being appointed to the important office of Public Orator. He then embarked on a political career and was elected as MP for Montgomeryshire, but suddenly changed course and in 1624 was ordained. He married in 1629, and the following year became rector of Bemerton, a parish in Wiltshire. He died in 1633.

The majority of his poems were written during his years as a country parson, and were published shortly after his death.

Herbert belongs to the group of poets later known as the '**metaphysical** poets'. Their poems were characterised by their use of unexpected comparisons and surprising imagery.

About the poem

Herbert's poems are mainly about his own experience of the Christian religious life and of the natural world. In this poem he describes some of the delightful things that he observes in the natural world. The thought that none of them lasts for ever causes him to reflect that only living virtuously leads to eternal life.

Virtue

Sweet day, so cool, so calm, so bright,
The bridal of the earth and sky:
The dew shall weep thy fall tonight,
For thou must die.

Sweet rose, whose hue angry and brave 5
Bids the rash gazer wipe his eye:
Thy root is ever in its grave,
And thou must die.

Sweet spring, full of sweet days and roses,
A box where sweets compacted lie: 10
My music shows ye have your closes,
And all must die.

Only a sweet and virtuous soul,
Like seasoned timber, never gives;
But though the whole world turn to coal, 15
Then chiefly lives.

GEORGE HERBERT
(1593–1633)

1 *sweet* – pleasing, sweet-smelling, pleasing to the ear, untainted, precious
2 *bridal* – wedding (metaphor)
5 *angry* – red
5 *brave* – striking, splendid
10 *sweets* – perfumes
10 *compacted* – packed close together
11 *music* – the poem's pattern
11 *closes* – ends of musical phrases
14 *gives* – yields
15 *coal* – ashes (at Day of Judgement)

Activities

Discussion and notemaking

Discuss these questions in pairs. Make notes of your answers, then share your ideas in a group discussion.

1. How does Herbert create in lines 1 and 2 a picture of a perfect spring day? What does the metaphor in line 2 suggest?

2. What feelings about the day's natural end does Herbert's use of personification in lines 3 and 4 suggest?
3. What feelings does Herbert suggest seeing a rose unexpectedly cause? Why does the person who sees it feel like this (lines 5 and 6)?
4. What do lines 7 and 8 say about the rose? How do they echo the thought in lines 3 and 4?
5. How do lines 9 and 10 draw together the delight Herbert experiences as he observes the natural world? How does the image he uses in line 10 convey the delights of spring?
6. What do the metaphor in line 11 and the statement in line 12 tell you about the person's feelings about things coming to an end in the natural world?
7. What comparison does Herbert use in the final verse, and what idea does this help him to convey?
8. How does verse 4 contrast with verses 1–3? Which words and phrases in this verse contrast most strongly with the language used in verses 1–3?

Speaking and listening

❧ In pairs, imagine you have been asked to contribute an item 'Thought for the Day' to a radio programme, and have chosen Herbert's poem. Discuss how you are going to introduce it, then draft the introduction and rehearse a reading of the poem. Form groups and compare your presentations of it.

Writing

❧ Draft either part of a sermon or a talk for assembly using Herbert's poem as your chosen text.

❧ Herbert wrote: 'Things of ordinary use serve for lights even of Heavenly Truth.' Explain how in his poem 'Virtue' Herbert uses observations of the natural world to express a religious point of view.

The Sick Rose

About the poet

For details of William Blake see page 121.

About the poem

This poem is from a book of Blake's poems published in 1794 entitled *Songs of Experience*. This book came five years after his *Songs of Innocence* (1789), poems in which he had expressed enjoyment of nature and pleasure in the uncorrupted things of life. In *Songs of Experience*, Blake writes poems about how innocence has been destroyed by man and society. In this poem he uses symbols in both the text and the illustration to reflect on an image of beauty being corrupted. The illustration is of Blake's etching from the book in which the poem was first published.

The Sick Rose

O Rose thou art sick.
The invisible worm
That flies in the night
In the howling storm:

Has found out thy bed 5
Of crimson joy:
And his dark secret love
Does thy life destroy.

WILLIAM BLAKE
(1757–1827)

Activities

Discussion and notemaking

On your own, make notes in response to these questions. Then share your ideas in a group discussion, amending and adding to your notes as you go.

1. Study Blake's etching before reading the poem. As your eye follows the rose bush from its root on the left to its flower on the centre right, what details do you notice?
2. Now read the poem and, as you study it, think about what it adds to what you have observed in the engraving. In verse 1, what do you think each of the following represents?
   - the rose
   - the worm
   - the night
   - the howling storm
3. Focus on verse 2. What do lines 5 and 6 suggest about the rose's condition even before the worm attacks it? What comment on human behaviour is suggested in the final two lines?

Speaking and listening

❧ On your own, draw the shape of a rose in the centre of a blank piece of paper. Pick out the key words and phrases from the poem and write them around the rose, drawing lines to connect them to the rose. Then brainstorm each word or phrase in turn, writing down any ideas you associate with them or images that they conjure up. Show each other your jottings and discuss them, before re-reading the poem and discussing any additional ideas about its meaning that have arisen from this activity.

Writing

❧ Use your notes to help you to draft an answer to this question, then compare your answers in groups.

'Explain how the poem and etching can be interpreted as more than a literal description of a rose being eaten by a worm.'

Ah! Sun-Flower

About the poet

For details of William Blake see page 121.

About the poem

This poem, like 'The Sick Rose' (see page 171), comes from Blake's collection of poems *Songs of Experience.* The poem is another fable, in which the sunflower is personified and used as a symbol to suggest human experience.

Before reading the poem remind yourself what personification is (see page 28).

Ah! Sun-Flower

Ah Sun-flower! weary of time,
Who countest the steps of the Sun,
Seeking after that sweet golden clime
Where the traveller's journey is done,

Where the Youth pined away with desire, 5
And the pale Virgin shrouded in snow,
Arise from their graves and aspire
Where my Sun-flower wishes to go.

WILLIAM BLAKE
(1757–1827)

3 *golden clime* – sky
6 *Virgin* – young woman
7 *aspire* – both 'ascend to' and 'long for' (in Blake's day)

Activities

Discussion and notemaking

Discuss these questions in groups, keeping notes of your ideas.

1. Discuss how in lines 1–4 Blake personifies the sunflower and uses its natural behaviour (sunflowers turn their heads as the sun moves, but remain firmly rooted in the earth) to suggest human experience. What are the 'sweet golden clime' (line 3) and 'the traveller's journey' (line 4)?
2. How do lines 5–6 suggest that human emotions, particularly those of the young, are restricted in this world?
3. In what way do lines 7–8 suggest that ultimately humans may achieve fulfilment?
4. What is the mood of this poem? Which of these words best sums up its mood? Can you suggest any others?
   - despair
   - consolation
   - acceptance
   - hope
   - dejection
   - optimism

Speaking and listening

❧ On your own, draw a rough sketch showing your design for a poster of this poem. Think carefully about the images that Blake includes in the poem and how you might illustrate them. Then, form groups and discuss your designs. Be prepared to revise your drawings in the light of other people's comments. Finally, share your ideas in a class discussion and choose a winning design.

Writing

❧ Discuss the imagery in 'Ah! Sun-Flower' which suggests that 'there is a golden world beyond and above the crippling world of experience'.

Up-hill

About the poet

For details of Christina Rossetti see page 7.

About the poem

This poem is an **allegory** – a piece of writing in which the characters and events are symbols of a moral or spiritual meaning. It was described by Rossetti's brother as 'a lively little song of the Tomb', but she had an answer for him: 'If sad and melancholy, I suggest that few people reach the age of 31 without sad and melancholy experiences.' When the poem was published in *Macmillan's Magazine* in February 1861 it won widespread praise, and led directly to the publication in the following year of *Goblin Market*, her first book of poems.

The poem is written as a dialogue, with alternate questions and answers.

Up-hill

Does the road wind up-hill all the way?
  Yes, to the very end.
Will the day's journey take the whole long day?
  From morn to night, my friend.

But is there for the night a resting-place? 5
  A roof for when the slow dark hours begin.
May not the darkness hide it from my face?
  You cannot miss that inn.

Shall I meet other wayfarers at night?
  Those who have gone before. 10
Then must I knock, or call when just in sight?
  They will not keep you standing at that door.

Shall I find comfort, travel-sore and weak?
  Of labour you shall find the sum.
Will there be beds for me and all who seek? 15
  Yea, beds for all who come.

Christina Rossetti
(1830–94)

14 *find the sum* – gain your reward

Activities

Discussion and notemaking

Discuss these questions in pairs. Make notes of your answers, then share your ideas in a group discussion.

1. Discuss the questions and the order in which they are asked. What do they suggest about the questioner?

2. How does the questioner react to the replies she receives? Do you think they

   - satisfy her?
   - alarm her?
   - confuse her?
   - reassure her?
   - depress her?

Give reasons for your views.

3. Discuss the poem's allegorical meaning.

   - Who are the two speakers, and what do they represent?
   - What are the 'road' (line 1) and what does the fact that it winds up-hill suggest?
   - What is 'the journey' (line 3)?
   - What are the 'resting-place' (line 5) and 'the inn' (line 8)?
   - Who are 'the other wayfarers' (line 9)?
   - What is the significance of the poem's last three questions and the replies that are given to them (lines 11–16)?

4. Do you think 'Up-hill' is a suitable title? Give your reasons. Discuss alternative titles and choose the one which you think is appropriate.

5. Which of these words most accurately sums up the mood of the poem? Can you suggest any others? Give reasons for your views.

   - sad
   - depressing
   - comforting
   - reassuring
   - threatening
   - anxious
   - melancholy
   - sombre
   - bleak
   - wistful
   - consoling

Speaking and listening

❧ In pairs, role play a scene in which a critic who has written a favourable review of the poem explains to Rossetti's brother why he considers it to be more than just 'a lively little song of the Tomb'.

❧ In pairs, practise different ways of reading the poem aloud. For example, depending on your tone you could make the questions simple open ones or anxious; and the replies could be either reassuring or threatening. When you have rehearsed your reading, form groups and compare your readings. Decide which reading is most effective and why.

Writing

❧ Explain how in 'Up-hill' Christina Rossetti uses an imagined conversation to present her reflections on life and the after-life.

No coward soul is mine

About the poet

For details of Emily Brontë see page 26.

About the poem

This poem was composed early in 1846, when Emily Brontë was writing *Wuthering Heights*. Cathy's words about Heathcliff in Chapter 9 of the novel are very similar to verses 5 and 6 where, as throughout the poem, 'thou' and 'thee' refer to God. 'I cannot express it; but surely you and every body have a notion that there is, or should be, an existence of yours beyond you. What were the use of my creation if I were entirely contained here? My great miseries in this world have been Heathcliff's miseries, and I watched and felt each from the beginning; my great thought in living is himself. If all else perished, and *he* remained, I should still continue to the end; and, if all else remained, and he were annihilated, the Universe would turn to a mighty stranger. I should not seem a part of it.'

No coward soul is mine

No coward soul is mine,
No trembler in the world's storm-troubled sphere:
I see Heaven's glories shine,
And Faith shines equal, arming me from Fear.

O God within my breast, 5
Almighty, ever-present Deity!
Life, that in me hast rest,
As I – Undying Life – have power in thee!

Vain are the thousand creeds
That move men's hearts: unutterably vain; 10
Worthless as withered weeds,
Or idlest froth amid the boundless main,

To waken doubt in one
Holding so fast by thy infinity;
So surely anchored on 15
The steadfast rock of Immortality.

With wide-embracing love
Thy spirit animates eternal years,
Pervades and broods above,
Changes, sustains, dissolves, creates and rears. 20

Though Earth and moon were gone
And suns and universes ceased to be,
And thou wert left alone
Every Existence would exist in thee.

There is not room for Death, 25
Nor atom that his might could render void,
Since thou art Being and Breath,
And what thou art may never be destroyed.

EMILY JANE BRONTË
(1818–48)

9 *vain* – useless
12 *main* – ocean
18 *animates* – inspires
23 *And* – If

Activities

Discussion and notemaking

Discuss these questions in pairs, and make notes of your answers. Then, share your ideas in a group discussion.

1. What do you learn about the poet's religious belief and how she feels it protects her (verse 1)?
2. What does she say about the strength her belief gives her (verse 2)?
3. What comparisons does she use in verses 3 and 4 to express her conviction that beliefs other than hers are powerless? List the words and phrases she uses to describe a) the weakness of other beliefs b) the strength of her own belief.
4. Discuss the eight verbs in verse 5 and comment on how each one helps to convey her belief in the might of God's love.
5. In your own words, explain the belief that Brontë expresses in verse 6.
6. What does she say about death and God's omnipotence in verse 7? Discuss how this verse brings her declaration of her belief to a climax.

Speaking and listening

❧ In pairs, discuss how people with different beliefs may respond to the poem. Then, develop a role play in which someone who, like the poet, has strong religious beliefs explains why she believes in God to someone who has no strong religious beliefs.

❧ In pairs, experiment with ways of reading this poem aloud in order to convey to your listeners the strength of the poet's faith and her total belief in the power of God.

Writing

❧ Write the journal entry that Emily Brontë might have made either before or after writing the poem, commenting on the thoughts and feelings she expresses in the poem.

❧ Trace the development of the poet's thinking in 'No coward soul is mine', and comment on how the structure of the poem and the language she uses help to convey the strength of her religious conviction.

❧ Compare what Brontë says in the poem with what is said in the extract from *Wuthering Heights* (see 'About the poem'). What do the two pieces of writing tell you about Brontë's emotions and thoughts?

Song

About the poet

For details of Christina Rossetti see page 7.

About the poem

In this poem, a person is addressing her lover about how she should like him to behave after her death.

Rossetti wrote this lyric just after her 18th birthday and her happy engagement to James Collinson. Its tone may have been influenced by her own ill-health and her father's sickness, for it reads as though she did not expect to live long enough to be married. In fact, the marriage never took place, not because she died, but because he became a Roman Catholic and she felt unable to marry him for religious reasons. However, giving the poem an autobiographical interpretation is only one of the ways in which it can be read.

Song

When I am dead, my dearest,
  Sing no sad songs for me;
Plant thou no roses at my head,
  Nor shady cypress tree:
Be the green grass above me 5
  With showers and dewdrops wet;
And if thou wilt, remember,
  And if thou wilt, forget.

I shall not see the shadows,
  I shall not feel the rain; 10
I shall not hear the nightingale
  Sing on, as if in pain:
And dreaming through the twilight
  That doth not rise nor set,
Haply I may remember, 15
  And haply may forget.

CHRISTINA ROSSETTI
(1830–94)

4 *cypress tree* – a symbol of mourning
15 *Haply* – perhaps

Activities

Discussion and notemaking

On your own, study the poem and make notes in answer to these questions. Then, compare your ideas in a group discussion.

1. In verse 1 how does the person in the poem request her lover to behave after her death?
2. In verse 2 what reasons does the person give for the requests she makes in the first verse?
3. What does verse 2 tell you about the person's attitude towards life after death?
4. What attitude do you think is shown in lines 15–16 to the love the two people shared?
5. Which word from this list best describes the mood of the person in the poem? Can you suggest any others?
   - serene
   - sentimental
   - whimsical
   - self-dramatising
   - consoling
   - unrealistic
   - tender
   - controlling

Speaking and listening

❧ In pairs, make notes for a reader suggesting how to read the poem aloud in order to bring out its tone, mood and musical qualities. Decide what effect you want your reading to have on listeners, and rehearse reading it in order to achieve that effect. Then choose some people to present their readings to the class, and discuss which reading is the most effective and why.

Writing

❧ Imagine the poem appeared in a newspaper as 'The Daily Poem'. Write an introduction saying why the poem has been chosen, commenting not only on what it says but also on its language and structure. Then, write a letter responding to it, either praising it because the writer of the letter approves of the ideas and feelings Rossetti expresses in the poem, or criticising it because the person disagrees with the sentiments Rossetti expresses.

Winged Words

About the poet

Mary Coleridge (1861–1907) was a descendant of the brother of the poet Samuel Taylor Coleridge (see page 124). She divided her time between teaching and writing, giving lessons on English literature at the Working Women's College and teaching working women in her own home. She wrote novels and poems and her poetry is sometimes compared with that of Emily Dickinson (see page 163).

About the poem

In this poem Mary Coleridge uses a single image to reflect upon the great impact made by the words poets write. The title 'Winged words' refers to poetry. It is derived from the idea that the source of poetic inspiration is Pegasus, a winged horse in Greek mythology.

Winged Words

As darting swallows skim across a pool,
  Whose tranquil depths reflect a tranquil sky,
So, o'er the depths of silence, dark and cool,
  Our wingèd words dart playfully,
    And seldom break 5
  The quiet surface of the lake,
    As they flit by.

MARY COLERIDGE
(1861–1907)

7 *flit* – fly rapidly

Activities

Discussion and notemaking

Study this poem on your own, make notes, then in pairs compare your ideas.

1. In what way are the words of poems like swallows? What does 'dart playfully' suggest? What are the 'depths of silence' (line 3)?
2. What does the poem suggest about the effect of the words poets write (lines 5–7)?
3. How would you describe the tone of the poem? Which word(s) from the list below do you think most accurately describes the tone of the poem? Can you suggest any others?
   - sardonic
   - jocular
   - ironic
   - dejected
   - cynical
   - morose
   - derisive
   - amused
   - wistful

Speaking and listening

❧ Role play an argument between two people, one of whom agrees with the views Mary Coleridge expresses about poetry and one of whom disagrees with her opinions.

Writing

❧ Write a similar poem of your own using a single image to express a contrasting view of the effect that words can have.
❧ Write an essay about poetry commenting on the way that poets use language to express their thoughts and feelings, and explaining how poems are different, both in form and effect, from prose. In your essay, use examples drawn from the poems in this book to support your argument.

General Questions

Before you begin answering a question, read each of the poems you are considering writing about. Look at the notes you made when you studied the poem previously, and then read the poem again. Then check that you

- understand what the poem means;
- can say something about your response to a) its tone, b) its language, c) its imagery, and d) its verse-form;
- have made up your mind about how the poem affects you;
- are ready to support or argue with the poem's theme.

If necessary, use the Glossary to check the meaning of any technical terms that you want to use when writing about the poem.

1. Compare the religious beliefs which are expressed in George Herbert's 'Virtue' and Emily Brontë's 'No coward soul is mine.' Discuss the language and imagery used in the poems and their different verse forms. Which poem do you think is the more effective? Give your reasons.

2. What attitude to life does Blake seem to you to express in his poems? Discuss how the imagery and symbolism in his poems help to convey his thoughts and feelings. (Refer to 'A Poison Tree' on page 121 and 'London' on page 155 as well as to 'The Sick Rose' and 'Ah! Sun-Flower'.)

3. What scene does Yeats describe in 'The Wild Swans at Coole' and Wordsworth describe in the extract from 'Lines Composed a Few Miles Above Tintern Abbey'? Compare how Yeats and Wordsworth use the description of a natural scene to explore their own feelings, commenting on the language and imagery they use.

4. Which of the poems in this section do you think most effectively conveys the poet's thoughts and feelings? Select *three* poems from the section which you found effective and compare them, commenting on the language, imagery, style and form of the poems. Explain which one you think is the most effective, and say why.

5. Choose *two* poems from this section which express contrasting attitudes to life. Write about the poems commenting on their form and structure, and on the techniques the poets use to convey their ideas.

Overview

The following questions are on poems from all the sections. Before you begin to answer a question, read each of the poems you are considering writing about. Look at the notes you made when you studied the poem previously, and then read the poem again. Then check that you

- understand what the poem means;
- can say something about your response to a) its tone, b) its language, c) its imagery, and d) its verse form;
- have made up your mind about how the poem affects you;
- are ready to support or argue with the poem's theme.

If necessary, use the Glossary to check the meaning of any technical terms that you want to use when writing about the poems.

1. Choose *two* poems and write about how they have made you think about your own beliefs and values.
2. Choose *two or three* poems about which people have disagreed because they have interpreted them differently. Write an essay focusing on these poems in which you argue against the opinion that 'every poem has only one meaning, if only you can find it'.
3. Compare *two* poems from the collection which you have found memorable because they have something to say about the experiences of life and death. Explain why you find them memorable.
4. Which poems would you select as good examples of the craft of poetry? Give reasons for your choices, and explain what you have learned about the craft of poetry-writing from studying the poems in this book.
5. Write a recommendation for another student with the title 'My top three classic poems'. Explain why you have chosen these three poems and the criteria you have used to make your selection.
6. Choose *two* poets whose poems you have responded to positively and *two* whose poems you have reacted to negatively. Explain the features of their poetry that led you either to like or dislike their poems.

Glossary

Cross references to other entries in the Glossary are in bold type.

adjective a word which adds to the meaning of a noun or pronoun, e.g. *cool green* house.

adverb a word which adds to the meaning of a **verb**, **adjective** or another adverb, e.g. grow *slowly*.

allegory a **narrative**, usually of some length, which is written to be read and understood to have a meaning beyond the literal (see 'Up-hill' page 174).

alliteration a sequence of repeated consonants, usually at the beginning of words (see page 18).

anapaest a three-syllable metrical **foot** in which two unstressed syllables are followed

× × /

by a stressed syllable, e.g. irrita(tion). Poets often choose it when wishing to give their lines a galloping **pace** (see Byron page 51). It is also used by Cowper (see page 136), where over-emphasising the **metre** when reading the poem aloud will distort its meaning.

Augustan used to describe writers from about the beginning to the middle of the eighteenth century. Their themes show a concern for the morality of both individuals and society, and their language is chosen to be polished and witty (see Dryden page 190, and Pope page 193). These writers looked back admiringly on the literature written in the reign of the Roman Emperor Augustus (27BC to AD14).

ballad a poem, usually written in a number of short verses, which narrates a story in simple, **colloquial** language. Many of the earliest ballads were spoken or sung, rather than written down. From the eighteenth century, poets have often chosen the ballad form for some of their poems about people and events, and these poems are known as *literary ballads* (see 'The Rime of the Ancient Mariner' page 124–5).

blank verse lines of unrhymed verse, each of ten syllables, and usually **iambic** (see Milton page 104, and Wordsworth, page 160).

coinage a word newly coined by and original to the poet (see Hopkins page 138).

colloquial language chosen to sound like ordinary conversation.

couplet two successive lines of verse rhyming together, and first used in English by Chaucer (see page 85). A couplet composed of two **iambic pentameters** (see Dryden page 90, and Pope page 93) is known as a **heroic couplet**.

dactyl a three-syllable metrical **foot** in which a stressed syllable is followed by two

/ × ×

unstressed ones, e.g. happily (see 'The Flowers of the Forest' page 49).

dialect a form of spoken English associated with an individual, region or class; it is different from Standard English (e.g. 'The Banks o' Doon' page 39–40).

diction the poet's choice of language. It may, for instance, be **colloquial** (see 'The Lament of the Demobilised' page 80) or elaborate (see 'Satan' page 104), or simple (see 'Song' page 179 and 'The Rime of the Ancient Mariner' page 124–5), with many original **coinages** (see 'Inversnaid' page 153) or full of **figurative language** (see 'Virtue' page 168).

dramatic monologue a poem in which an imaginary speaker, not the poet, is portrayed addressing an audience (see Browning's 'My Last Duchess' page 95–6).

Elizabethan literature written during the reign of Queen Elizabeth 1 (1558–1603), a period when new verse forms, such as the **sonnet** and **blank verse**, were developed in English, and when Shakespeare (see page 28), Jonson (see page 165) and Marlowe (see page 16) were writing plays as well as poems. Other poets included Sidney and Spenser.

epic a long **narrative** poem written in formal language about the exploits of superhuman heroes. The earliest *traditional epics* were part of the oral tradition of a nation; later, *literary epics* were written by a single poet for an audience able to read them, e.g. 'Paradise Lost' (see page 104–5).

epitaph an inscription on a tomb, or a literary farewell which may be serious or witty. The most effective epitaphs are short.

fable a short **narrative** in prose or poetry which conveys a clear moral lesson. The characters are usually inanimate or non-human creatures.

feminine ending/rhyme a word of two or more syllables, the last of which is not stressed. When two of these words are rhymed it is called a *feminine rhyme* (see 'The evening darkens over' page 45 and 'On Wenlock Edge' page 133-4).

figurative language language which uses figures of speech to enrich its meaning. The most common are **metaphors** (see page 17) and **similes** (see page 26). Vivid **imagery** is usually prominent in it.

foot a unit of two or three **syllables** which joins with others to make up a line of poetry. See **anapaestic**, **dactylic**, **iambic**.

free verse poetry with neither regular **metre** nor length of line, i.e. poetry which is free of the patterns of traditional poetry (see 'A Woman to Her Lover' page 24–5). The American poet Walt Whitman (1819–92) was the first to use it for most of his poetry. It has become widely used in the twentieth century.

Georgian an adjective used to describe the poetry of the early part of the reign of George V (1910–36). Its **verse forms** were usually traditional, and its subjects drawn from the countryside. Brooke, Sassoon and Owen at first wrote poetry of this kind, but changed utterly under the influence of the events of the First World War (1914–18).

half-rhyme in words which are rhymed, the vowels, and sometimes consonants too, are chosen because they do not exactly match. This deliberate effect can be seen in Owen (page 78).

heroic couplet a pair of **iambic pentameters**, rhyming together.

hexameter a line consisting of six metrical feet.

iambic a term used to describe a two-syllable unit of **metre**, or **foot**, in which an unstressed syllable is followed by a stressed
× /
syllable, e.g. alive. It is the commonest aural pattern in English poetry (see Shakespeare page 28).

image a picture created in the mind by the poet's words and the ideas they suggest.

imagery refers to a poem's **figurative language**, especially its **metaphors** and **similes.**

irony a statement which says one thing but for an alert reader means something else (see the last two lines of 'George Villiers' page 93).

language when you are asked to comment on the *language* of a poem, you need to pick out characteristics which are striking or unusual, e.g. 'Inversnaid' page 153, 'There Came a Wind like a Bugle' page 163.

lyric a tuneful poem expressing in a personal way the thoughts and feelings of an individual (not necessarily the poet). The term is derived from the Greek word *lyrikos*, meaning a poem to be sung to the lyre (a small harp).

metaphor a figure of speech which describes a person or object by comparing, for a particular purpose, that person or object with something else (see page 7).

metaphysical an adjective used to describe a number of seventeenth-century poets, such as Donne, Herbert (see page 167) and Marvell. Their poetry often uses simple or **colloquial** language, often marked by wordplay and surprising **imagery**. They invented a large number of original **stanza** forms.

metre the pattern of stressed and unstressed syllables in a line of poetry. The commonest metre in English is the **iambic** (see 'To My Dear and Loving Husband' page 22). Other metres often used are the **anapaestic** (see 'The Destruction of Sennacherib' page 51), where two unstressed syllables are followed by one stressed, and **dactylic** (see 'The Flowers of the Forest' page 49), where the stressed syllable is followed by two unstressed ones.

mood the emotional character of a poem; also the kind of effect a speaker wishes to make on an audience when reading the poem aloud.

narrative a narrative is a story; a narrator, the person who tells the story.

octave the first section, of eight lines, of a Petrarchan **sonnet** (see page 12).

onomatopoeia words chosen because they sound like the noise they describe (see line 6 of 'Suicide in the Trenches' page 72, and lines 30–33 of 'To Autumn' page 128).

pace the rate of speed which the **rhythm** of a poem creates; also, the rate of speed at which a reader decides the lines of a poem should be spoken.

paradox a statement which appears to contradict itself, but in fact makes sense; often used by the **Metaphysical** Poets.

parody a poem which is written in imitation of the style of another poem. Its aim is to ridicule the original poem's characteristics, especially its **language** (see 'The Nymph's Reply to the Shepherd' page 20 and 'Another Epitaph on an Army of Mercenaries' page 60). When a poem is written in the style of another without intending mockery, it is known as a *pastiche*.

pastoral literature describing an imaginary, simple and idealised world in which shepherds and shepherdesses fall in love, often to music (see 'The Passionate Shepherd to His Love' page 16–17).

pentameter a line of verse composed of five metrical feet. The **iambic** pentameter is the most common metre in English, occurring either as **heroic couplets** (see 'Thomas Shadwell' page 90), or, unrhymed, as **blank verse** (as in Shakespeare's plays and 'Ulysses' page 106–8).

personification an animal, object or idea is referred to as though it is a person (see page 28).

quatrain a **stanza** of four lines which may be rhymed or unrhymed. It is the commonest **verse form** in English.

rhetorical question a sentence, written as a question, but not expecting a reply. Writers often use it to express surprise (e.g. Macbeth's 'Is this a dagger which I see before me?') or a problem which is unanswerable (see the last two lines of 'The Wild Swans at Coole' page 158–9).

rhyme the repetition, in the rhyming words, of their last stressed vowel and any following sounds (see 'The evening darkens over' page 45 and 'Porphyria's Lover' page 36–7).

rhyme scheme the pattern of rhymes in a **stanza** or poem. You can describe it by giving each rhyme a lower-case letter, e.g. abab (see page 7).

rhythm our sense of the movement made in a line of poetry by the arrangement of stressed and unstressed syllables.

Romantic an adjective used to describe literature written between about 1789 and 1830. The **Romantic** Poets tended to value a person's capacity for feeling more than thinking (see Blake page 121), and the individual and his freedom more than society and its rules (see 'London' page 155 and 'Tintern Abbey' page 161). Wordsworth and Coleridge argued for the use of simplified **diction** in poetry ('a selection of the language actually used by men'), which they defined in *Lyrical Ballads* (see pages 124, 160) as the 'spontaneous overflow of powerful feelings'. Many of the poets supported the ideals of the 1789 Revolution in France and other revolutionary politics (for example Blake, Byron, Shelley).

run-on a line of poetry whose construction runs into the next line without a grammatical break (see 'My Last Duchess' lines 2–4, 15–22).

satire writing which portrays a person's foolishness and wickedness so as to make them appear ridiculous or contemptible. It is poetry of protest (see 'Thomas Shadwell' page 90 and 'George Villiers' page 93).

sestet the final section, of six lines, of a Petrarchan **sonnet** (see page 12).

simile a figure of speech in which comparison is made between two people or things using 'like' or 'as' (see page 26).

sonnet a rhyming **lyric** poem of 14 **iambic pentameters**. The main **rhyme schemes** are the Shakespearian (see page 28) and the Petrarchan (see page 12).

Spenserian stanza a verse form invented by Edmund Spenser for his poem 'The Faerie Queene' (1589). It has nine **iambic** lines, the first eight being **pentameters** and the last an alexandrine (an iambic **hexameter**). The rhyme scheme is ababbcbcc.

sprung rhythm a term invented by Gerard Manley Hopkins to describe the system of **metre** in his own poems (see page 138).

stanza a grouping of the individual verse lines in a poem, often marked by a regular and repeating pattern of **rhymes**. In a printed text, one stanza is marked off from the next by a space.

style the characteristic way in which a poem is written; also, how a particular poet writes. Important features include a poet's choice of subject matter, **language**, **imagery**, **rhyme schemes** and **stanza** structure.

stress the emphasis put on a syllable by speaking it more firmly than a syllable which is not stressed. In any line of metrical poetry there will be a pattern of stressed and unstressed syllables.

syllable a unit of sound which forms a word or part of a word. For example, 'hand' has one syllable, 'hand-some' has two syllables, and 'hand-ker-chief' three.

symbol an object used in a poem to stand for something else; an idea is combined with a picture. Thus, a pair of scales is a symbol for justice; a rose for beauty (see 'The Sick Rose' page 171)

theme a poem's main idea. For example, the theme of 'George Villiers' (page 93) is that a life led selfishly and immorally will end in unhappiness, whilst in 'Virtue' (page 168) Herbert's theme is the reward of living a Christian life; the theme of 'The Slave Mother' (page 110–11) is the suffering caused by, and therefore the inhumanity of slavery; the theme of 'Binsey Poplars' (page 139) is our duty to respect/preserve the environment.

tone the manner or **mood** of a poem and the way in which it must be understood and spoken aloud. It may be, for example, angry (see 'Suicide in the Trenches' page 72), sad (see 'The Slave Mother' page 110–11), ironic (see 'George Villiers' page 93). When a reader does not notice irony, the writer's meaning will be completely misunderstood (see 'The Prioress' page 86–9).

trochee a two-syllable metrical **foot** in which a stressed syllable is followed by an unstressed one, e.g. stubborn (see 'It was night and on the mountains' page 150 and 'A Poison Tree' page 121).

verb a word indicating an action, state or event, forming the main part of the predicate of a sentence. The poet's choice of an exact or surprising verb often helps to create a striking image, e.g. stanza 1 of 'To Autumn' page 127.

verse form the **metre** and **stanza** patterns chosen to help in creating the poem. There is a close link between the poet's form and meaning, e.g. 'Dover Beach' page 147–8, and 'Binsey Poplars' page 139.

verse paragraph part of a poem dealing with a particular topic or point of view. It is a unit because of its meaning, not because of its **verse form** (see 'A Woman to Her Lover' page 24–5).

Victorian an adjective used to describe the literature of the reign of Queen Victoria (1837–1901). It was a great period in the development of the English novel, and also produced a wide range of important poetry. Much of it is about contemporary social problems, many connected with the effects of the Industrial Revolution (see Thomas Hood page 113–15).

Chronology of Poets

Index of First Lines